HAIKUS
OF
ALL SEASONS III

FAUNA

MAYUMI ITOH

In memory of the animals

who became victims of World War II and other wars

and

Hachi-kō (November 1923–March 1935)

Contents

Note for paperback edition: This book is for on-demand printing. The actual page numbers (and page breaks and other formatting matters) may differ from the page numbers shown in the Table of Contents above, due to the formatting by Amazon that is used on the day of the book order.

List of photographs

Sources for all photographs are credited below except for those that were taken by the author.

Photograph 1. "Soul of Dog" Shrine, under Wikimedia Commons license, "Reiken Shrine," July 8, 2010, https://commons.wikimedia.org/wiki/File:霊犬神社_-_panoramio_(1).jpg

Photograph 2. Black headed gull, under Wikimedia Commons license, "Larus ridibundus black headed gull, Hiranai, Aomori, Japan," December 26, 2007, https://commons.wikimedia.org/wiki/File:Larus_ridibundus_Black_headed_Gull_Hiranai_Aomori_Japan.jpg

Photograph 3. Dog pilgrimage to Ise Grand Shrine, under Wikimedia Commons license, "Tokaidō Fifty-Three

Photograph 6. Canada geese and goslings crossing the

street by a lake, taken by the author

Photograph 7. Turtles sunbathing, taken by the author

Photograph 8. Chinese tropical fritillary butterfly, Komaki

Citizens' Forest for Four Seasons, Komaki, Aichi

prefecture, August 2010, taken by the author

Photograph 9. Red spider lily, under Wikimedia Commons

license, "Cluster amaryllis close-up," September 19, 2004,

https://commons.wikimedia.org/wiki/File:Cluster_amaryllis

_close-up.jpg

Photograph 10. School of fish, projected on wall, Kaneno

Misuzu Memorial Museum, Nagato, Yamaguchi prefecture,

August 2012, taken by the author

Photograph 11. Cover of *Gon gitsune* (Gon, the Little Fox),

© Kuroi Ken, written by Niimi Nankichi (first published in

1932) and aesthetically and poetically illustrated by Kuroi

Ken (Kaiseisha: Tokyo, 1986), taken by the author

Photograph 12. Red-crowned cranes, under Wikimedia

Commons license, "Red-crowned cranes, Hokkaido,

Japan," February 20, 2011,

https://commons.wikimedia.org/wiki/File:Red-

crowned_Cranes_-_Hokkaido_-

_Japan_S4E4202_(15525814846).jpg

Notes on the Text

This book presents each haiku in both Japanese and English so that non-Japanese-speaking readers can fully appreciate it. The first page for a given haiku (on the left side) shows the original haiku in Japanese, which is made up of a combination of Chinese characters (*kanji*) and Japanese phonetic characters (*hiragana* and *katakana*). In accordance with the customs for writing haiku, the old spellings of *hiragana* are used for the original haiku.

Then, in order to facilitate a better understanding, especially for those who are studying Japanese, the original haiku is shown in a modern spelling in *hiragana* and *katakana*. This allows readers to see how the haiku is exactly pronounced phonetically. There are many ways to pronounce specific *kanji* words, and the original Japanese haiku does not indicate how each *kanji* word is actually pronounced. It is sometimes difficult even for Japanese

readers to know the pronunciation. Therefore, the simpler
rendition of each haiku only in modern *hiragana* and
katakana will help.

Afterward, the identification of the season word for
the haiku is given and some explanations of the cultural and
historical backgrounds are added where applicable.

On the second page for a given haiku (on the right
side), a romanization of the original Japanese haiku is
provided, first, so that English-speaking readers can
understand how the haiku is pronounced. The words in
Roman letters are divided into smaller groups of syllables,
for easier reading.

Then, an English translation of the haiku is
presented. It is a paraphrasing of the haiku, rather than a
literal translation, in order for it to make the best sense in
English. Accordingly, for many cases, the word order of
the haiku might be different from the original haiku in
Japanese. It is followed by the English translations of the

season word and the explanations of the cultural and historical backgrounds. This completes the presentation of a given haiku.

All translations, including those of haikus, were made by the author. For romanizing Japanese words, the Hepburn style is primarily used, with macrons. However, macrons are not used for words known in English without macrons, as for Kyoto and Tokyo. Another exception is that "n" is not converted to "m" for words where it precedes "b, m, and p." Examples include tonbo, instead of tombo; Gunma prefecture, instead of Gumma prefecture; and tanpopo, instead of tampopo.

Names of Japanese persons are given with the surname first, except for those who use the reversed order in English. Honorific prefixes, such as doctor and mister, are not used in the text, except in direct quotations.

Acknowledgments

I would like to thank all the members of the *Hoshi no shima kukai* (the Haiku Society of Star Island, a new name for the Haiku Society of New York), past and present—including but not limited to Esaka Kinuyo, Hara Yasuko, Sakuhara Aya, and Tsukino Popona—as well as Tsuneo Akaha, Kent Calder, Toshiko Calder, Steve Clemons, Akiko Collcutt, Gerald Curtis, Joshua Fogel, Hoshi Hiroshi, Ronald Hrebenar, Ken Kawata, Donald Keene, Ellis Krauss, Mike Mochizuki, T. J. Pempel, Stephen Roddy, Gilbert Rozman, Richard Samuels, Vicki Wong, Donald Zagoria, and Quansheng Zhao, for continuous encouragement and inspirations. I extend my deep appreciation to Gregory Rewoldt and Meg Itoh for generous support.

Preface

This is the third haiku anthology by this author and is
dedicated to the animals who became victims of World
War II and other wars, as well as to two Akita-inus, in
association with the Year of the Dog, 2018: Hachi-kō
(circa November 14, 1923–March 8, 1935) and Wasao (b.
circa summer 2007), who touched the hearts of millions of
people worldwide.

This anthology is also a tribute to the people who
have committed themselves to the protection and welfare of
animals. They include Nagoya City Higashiyama Zoo first
director Kitaō Hideichi (July 1900–December 1993), who
resisted the Japanese government Wartime Disposal of
Dangerous Animals order the longest among the zoos
nationwide and resigned his position in June 1945, and
Tokyo Zoological Park Society second president Takasaki
Tatsunosuke (February 1885–February 1964), who after the
Soviet Army invasion of Manchuria in August 1945 not

only voluntarily stayed there and toiled to repatriate Japanese civilians, but also devoted himself to animals there and elsewhere.

For rules about haiku making, please see *Haikus of All Seasons I: The Heavens and The Earth* (2018). For background information, please read *Japanese Wartime Zoo Policy: The Silent Victims of World War II* (2010); *Hachiko: Solving Twenty Mysteries about the Most Famous Dog in Japan* (2017); Vicki Wong & Hachi: A Dog's Tale (the true story of the loyal dog Hachikō), https://www.facebook.com/groups/vickiwongandhachi; Hachi & Friends group, https://www.facebook.com /groups/379220079122446; and Wasao's Facebook page, https://www.facebook.com/wasao.official.

合掌 (gasshō), the Japanese equivalent of RIP

Japanese "Be Kind to Animals Week"

September 20–September 26, 2018

January

Photograph 1. "Soul of Dog" Shrine, under Wikimedia

Commons license, "Reiken Shrine," July 8, 2010,

https://commons.wikimedia.org/wiki/File:霊犬神社_-

panoramio(1).jpg

初詣

　　犬の参拝

　　　　「犬神社」

はつもうで

　　いぬのさんぱい

　　　　いぬじんじゃ

季語　　初詣（新年）

2018年は戌年。近年、ペットブームに伴い、犬のお祓い・
祈祷を行う「犬神社」が増えつつある。

Hatsu mōde

>inu no sanpai

>>"inu jinsha"

On New Year's Day

>the dog visits

>>the Dog Shrine

Season word: *hatsu mōde* (a visit to a shrine on New Year's Day; signifies new year)

2018 is the Year of the Dog according to the Chinese zodiac calendar. In recent years, Shinto shrines have created "dog shrines" specifically designed for offering prayer services for dogs.

初詣

　　ご祈祷待つ犬

　　　　並びたり

はつもうで

　　ごきとうまついぬ

　　　　ならびたり

季語　初詣（新年）

Hatsu mōde

gokitō matsu inu

narabi tari

On a visit to a shrine on New Year's Day

dogs are lining up

waiting to be prayed for and purified

Season word: *hatsu mōde* (a visit to a shrine on New

Year's Day; new year)

初雪や

　　　生き物の描く

　　　　　水墨画

はつゆきや

　　　いきもののかく

　　　　　すいぼくが

季語　初雪（冬）

初雪の上に残る鹿や兎の足跡が水墨画を描いたような様子は清々しくも趣き深い。

Hatsu yuki ya

    ikimono no kaku

        suiboku ga

On the first snow

    wildlife have drawn

        a black-and-white wash painting

Season word: *hatsu yuki* (first snow of the season; winter)

The footprints of wildlife on the first snow of the year look like a black-and-white wash painting.

「砂嵐」

　　椰子の木陰に

　　　寄る駱駝

すなあらし

　　やしのこかげに

　　　よるらくだ

季語　「砂嵐」（1991年1月17日の「砂漠の嵐作戦」、冬）

「砂嵐」は、湾岸戦争中、1991年1月17日に開始された

米軍を中心とする多国籍軍のイラク空爆、「砂漠の嵐作戦」

のこと。

"Suna arashi"

yashi no kokage ni

yoru rakuda

The camel takes refuge

under the coconut tree

during Desert Storm

Season word: *"Suna arashi"* (Operation Desert Storm,

January 17, 1991; winter)

This is an image from Operation Desert Storm in Iraq of

the coalition forces led by the U.S. Army, which began on

January 17, 1991.

ハチ公や

　　吹雪の大館

　　　永遠に去る

ハチこうや

　　ふぶきのおおだて

　　　とわにさる

季語　吹雪(冬)

「渋谷のハチ公」は、1923年11月14日頃秋田県北秋田郡二井田村大子内(現在の大館市)で生まれた。大吹雪の1924年1月14日、生後二ヶ月になったハチは、小型の米俵に入れられ、蒸気機関車で東京へ送られた。丸一日かかった「一人旅」は子犬にとってはきついものであり、上野駅に着いた時は死んでいるかと思われたほどであった。

Hachi kō ya

    fubuki no Ōdate

        towa ni saru

In the blizzard

    Hachi-kō left his birthplace

    Ōdate forever

Season word: *fubuki* (blizzard; winter)

The Akita-inu Hachi-kō was born in the snow country Ōdate,

Akita prefecture, around November 14, 1923. On January 14,

1924, the two-month old puppy left his birthplace in a blizzard,

never to return. He traveled alone on the Ōu Main Line

connecting to the Tōhoku Main Line and arrived at Ueno Station

in Tokyo the next day. It was an arduous trip for the puppy and

people thought he was dead when he arrived in Tokyo.

ハチ公や

　　道玄坂を

　　　　橇のごと

ハチこうや

　　どうげんざかを

　　　　そりのごと

季語　橇（そり、冬）

ハチ公の飼主、上野英三郎（1872年–1925年）の妻八重は、「ハ
チは冬の散歩中、雪の積もった坂道を仰向けになって雪滑りをし
た。その姿がおかしくて、私達を笑わせた。」と語った。「ハチ公」は、
他人のつけた愛称で、本当の名前はハチ。ハチ公ファンページ:
Vicki Wong & Hachi: A Dog's Tale, https://www.facebook.
com/groups/vickiwongandhachi; Hachi & Friends group,
https://www.facebook.com/groups/379220079122446.

Hachi kō ya

Dōgenzaka o

sori no goto

Hachi-kō is sledding

down Dōgenzaka hill

like a sleigh

Season word: *sori* (sleigh; winter)

Hachi-kō enjoyed sliding downhill during winter. Yae, the widow

of Hachi's owner, Ueno Hidesaburō (1872–1925) stated, "Hachi

(Hachi-kō's real name) slid on the snow face-up and deftly

maneuvered his body by steering with his head and legs. This made

us laugh." Hachi's Facebook pages: Vicki Wong & Hachi: A Dog's

Tale, https://www.facebook.com/groups/vickiwongandhachi; Hachi &

Friends group, https://www.facebook.com/groups/379220079122446

軽トラに

　　聴き耳立てる

　　　　犬と雪

けいトラに

　　ききみみたてる

　　　　いぬとゆき

季語　　雪（冬）

青森県津軽郡鰺ヶ沢町でイカ焼き店を経営していた菊谷節子は、2008年頃、捨てられていた長毛の秋田犬を保護し、レオと名付けた。その後、わさおと改名されたその犬を全国的に有名にしたが、2017年11月30日に亡くなった（享年73歳）。わさおは菊谷にしか懐かなかった。菊谷の死後、わさおは家の前の道路を軽トラックが通る度に注視してやまない。菊谷が生前、軽トラックを運転していたため。

Kei tora ni

kiki mimi tateru

inu to yuki

The dog and the snow

are carefully listening

to the mini trucks driving in the street

Season word: *yuki* (snow; winter)

The "dog" refers to an Akita-inu Wasao (b. c. summer 2007) in

Ajigasawa, Tsugaru county, Aomori prefecture. He was a stray

and was adopted by the local broiled squid shop proprietress

Kikuya Setsuko. Wasao became nationally popular, but he

opened up only to Kikuya. After she had died on November 30,

2017, Wasao kept watching the street and checked every mini

truck driving by in the street. Kikuya used to drive a mini truck.

大吹雪

　　つばき庇ひて

　　　往くわさお

おおふぶき

　　つばきかばいて

　　　いくわさお

季語　大吹雪（冬）

菊谷節子は、以前入院した際、わさおの食欲が減り、10

キロも痩せてしまったのを見て、自分が死んだ後わさおが

生きていけるように、わさおにお嫁さんを捜した。2014年

10月、当時2才の秋田犬つばきがわさおのお嫁さんとなる。

その甲斐あって、菊谷亡き後、わさおはつばきを伴侶に懸

命に生きている。

Ō fubuki

    Tsubaki kabai te

        iku Wasao

In the blizzard

    Wasao protects Tsubaki

        and leads in the dog walk

Season word: *Ō-fubuki* (blizzard; winter)

When Kikuya Setsuko was hospitalized, Wasao stopped eating and lost 20 pounds. Having realized this, Kikuya found him a mate, a two-year-old Akita-inu Tsubaki (*lit.*, "camellia"), so that Wasao would not be devastated too much after Kikuya's death. Today, Wasao is coping with her death. Her plan worked.

犬啼きて

　　寒椿落ち

　　　雪の泣く

いぬなきて

　　かんつばきおち

　　　ゆきのなく

季語　寒椿(冬)　雪(冬)

菊谷節子追悼。

Inu naki te

kan tsubaki ochi

yuki no naku

The dog cried

the winter camellia fell

and the snow wept

Season words: *kan tsubaki* (winter camellia, *camellia hiemalis*; winter) and *yuki* (snow; winter)

Kikuya Setsuko picked up a long-haired Akita-inu on the street and adopted him. The dog became Wasao. He was probably abandoned by a breeder, as a long-haired Akita-inu was considered undesirable. The pedigree Akita-inu is supposed to be short-haired. The popularity of Wasao is owed to Kikuya.

秋田犬

　　　大地の雪を

　　　　　踏みしめて

あきたいぬ

　　　だいちのゆきを

　　　　　ふみしめて

季語　雪（冬）

菊谷節子亡き後、力強く生きるわさお。

わさお公式ファンページ:

https://www.facebook.com/wasao.official

Akita inu

    daichi no yuki o

        fumi shime te

The Akita-inu

    is firmly stepping on the deep snow

        in the snow country

Season word: *yuki* (snow; winter)

Wasao lives in the Tsugaru region, the snow country of Japan. Wasao walks in the deep snow and shows his resolve to live after his owner's death. Wasao's Facebook page is https://www.facebook.com/wasao.official.

February

Photograph 2. Black headed gull, under Wikimedia

Commons license, "Larus ridibundus black headed gull,

Hiranai, Aomori, Japan," December 26, 2007,

https://commons.wikimedia.org/wiki/File:Larus_ridibundus

_Black_headed_Gull_Hiranai_Aomori_Japan.jpg

百合鴎

　　凍し湖面の

　　　　姿見ゆ

ゆりかもめ

　　いてしこめんの

　　　　すがたみゆ

季語　百合鴎（ユリカモメ、冬）

湖面に映る自分の美しい姿に見入る百合鴎。ユリカモメは、秋に日本に渡来し越冬する冬鳥。白い体羽、赤い嘴と脚、目の後ろの黒い斑点が特徴。夏羽は、頭部が黒褐色になる（英語名の由来）。魚が主食。

Yuri kamome

    iteshi komen no

        sugata miyu

The black-headed gull

    is looking at its reflection

        in the frozen lake

Season word: *yuri kamome* (*lit.*, "[white] lily gull," black-headed gull; winter)

The black-headed gull signifies winter as it migrates and winters in Japan. Its red beak and feet, with its white body plumage, makes it an attractive bird. The color of its head plumage turns black in summer; hence the English name.

産声や

　　ハチ公雪を

　　　駆け回る

うぶごえや

　　ハチこうゆきを

　　　かけまわる

季語　雪(冬)

ハチ公の飼い主、上野英三郎には公には子供がいないと
されているが、実は息子がいた。妻の八重によると、ハチ
が一歳(数え年)の時、夫婦に長男が生まれた。八重は、
「ハチは、赤ちゃんの誕生に大喜びした」と語っている。

Ubu goe ya

 Hachi kō yuki o

  kake mawaru

Hearing the first cry of the newborn baby

 Hachi-kō ran around the garden

  in the snow with joy

Season word: *yuki* (snow; winter)

In official records, Hachi's owner, Ueno Hidesaburō (1872–
1925), did not have any children. However, according to his
widow, Yae, they had a son when Hachi was a year old (in the
traditional age counting, which corresponds to being under one
year old). Hachi was excited with the birth of the baby. For
details, see https://www.amazon.com/HACHIKO-SOLVING-
TWENTY-MYSTERIES-FAMOUS/dp/1973380137.

日向ぼこ

　　赤児に添ひ寝の

　　　　ハチ公

ひなたぼこ

　　あかごにそいねの

　　　　ハチこう

季語　日向ぼこ（冬）

ハチ公の飼い主、上野英三郎の妻の八重によると、ハチが一歳（数え年）の時、夫婦には長男が生まれたが、「ハチはその赤ちゃんが大好きで、一緒に昼寝をさせるととても喜んだ」という。

Hinata boko

    akago ni soine no

        Hachi kō

Basking in the winter sun

    Hachi-kō is taking a nap

        with the newborn baby

Season word: *hinata boko* (winter sunbathing; winter)

Ueno Hidesaburō's widow Yae stated, "Hachi truly enjoyed a company of our newborn son. He seemed to be very happy when we let him take a nap with the baby."

シベリアの

　　流氷渡り

　　　跳びし犬

シベリアの

　　りゅうひょうわたり

　　　とびしいぬ

季語　流氷（春）

第二次世界大戦後、シベリアに抑留された日本人捕虜に
匿われ、1956年12月25日、最後の帰還船に乗船した帰
還兵を追って流氷に飛び込んだ野良犬、クロの実話にち
なんで。

Shiberia no

ryūhyō watari

tobi shi inu

The dog jumped onto

and crossed the floating ice

in Siberia

Season word: *ryūhyō* (floating ice; spring)

This refers to the true story of the dog called Kuro (*lit.*, "black"),

who was adopted by the Japanese POWs detained in a

concentration camp in Siberia after the end of World War II. In

December 1956, when their repatriation finally came about,

Kuro jumped onto the sea of ice, chasing after their ship. He

was rescued and was "repatriated" with the soldiers. Their story

is available at https://www.amazon.com/Hachi-kō-Siberia-Story-

Japanese-Prisoners/dp/1521708894.

水俣の春

　　猫踊り

　　　狂ひたり

みなまたのはる

　　ねこおどり

　　　くるいたり

季語　　春（春）

初の公害とされる熊本県の水俣病。水銀に汚染された魚を食べた猫が真っ先に犠牲となり、狂ったように踊って死んでいった（猫踊り病）。2月22日は「猫の日」。

Minamata no haru

neko odori

kurui tari

Spring in Minamata

the cat went mad

and danced a "mad cat dance"

Season word: *haru* (spring; spring)

In the early 1950's, cats in Minamata, Kumamoto prefecture,

acted strangely as if mad, which local folk referred to as the

"mad cat dance," and died. They had eaten fish contaminated by

industrial waste dumped in the sea. They suffered from mercury

poisoning. This became known as the Minamata Disease. The

cats were like 'canaries in a coal mine.'

不知火の

　　春の漁り火

　　　猫の哭く

しらぬいの

　　はるのいさりび

　　　ねこのなく

季語　　春（春）

2018年2月10日に亡くなった石牟礼道子（1927年-20

18年）追悼。石牟礼は水俣で猫に接することによって地

元漁村の異変に気づき、水俣病患者の救済に尽くす。不

知火（八代海）の漁師は猫と共存してきた。漁に猫を連れ

て行き、猫に漁具を荒らす鼠を取らせ、褒美に魚を与えた。

猫と共に漁師も水銀中毒の犠牲となった。

Shiranui no

   haru no isaribi

    neko no naku

In Shiranui

   under the spring fires of fishermen to lure fish

    one finds the cat weeping in mourning

Season word: *haru* (spring; spring)

This is a memorial tribute to Ishimure Michiko (1927–2018),

who died on February 10, 2018. The Shiranui (Yatsushiro) Sea

is the inner sea of Minamata. She noticed the mercury poisoning

in Minamata by observing the strange behavior of the local cats

and became the major advocate for the victims of the Minamata

Disease. The class-action lawsuits still go on.

春の宵

　　猫の孤島や

　　　　恋の島

はるのよい

　　ねこのことうや

　　　　こいのしま

季語　　春の宵（春）

近年、宮城県にある田代島（たしろじま）や福岡県の相島
（あいのしま）などが、「猫の島」、「猫の楽園」として観光客
の間で人気を集めている。

Haru no yoi

    neko no kotō ya

        koi no shima

In the spring evening

    the Cat Island has become

        the Island of Love

Season word: *haru no yoi* (spring evening; spring)
There are several "Cat Islands," such as Ainoshima, Fukuoka prefecture, and Tashirojima, Miyagi prefecture, which are underpopulated by people and are overpopulated by cats. In recent years, they have become popular tourist destinations.

梅の香や

　　わさおの心

　　　　綻びて

うめのかや

　　わさおのこころ

　　　　ほころびて

季語　　梅（春）

唯一人懐いていた菊谷節子が亡くなって3ヶ月以上が経

ち、北国の津軽地方にもようやく春の兆しが現れ、わさお

の心を慰める。

Ume no ka ya

Wasao no kokoro

hokorobi te

The scent of plum blossoms

opens up

the heart of Wasao

Season word: *ume* (plum blossoms; spring)

More than three months have passed since the death of
Kikuya Setsuko, to whom the long-haired Akita-inu Wasao
only opened up. The plum buds have opened in the snow
country of Tsugaru and console Wasao.

春再び

　　津軽の犬の

　　　　親善大使

はるふたたび

　　つがるのいぬの

　　　　しんぜんたいし

季語　　春（春）

2010年6月、秋田犬のわさおは青森県鰺ヶ沢町の特別

観光大使に任命される。さらに、2011年2月には、日本ユ

ネスコ協会連盟の「世界遺産活動特別大使犬」に任命さ

れ、東日本大地震後は、JR鰺ヶ沢駅駅長などを務め、募

金活動に寄与した。

Haru futatabi

Tsugaru no inu no

shinzen taishi

Spring has come again

and the Akita-inu of Tsugaru

has become a goodwill ambassador

Season word: *haru* (spring; spring)

In June 2010, the long-haired Akita-inu Wasao was appointed as

a special tourism ambassador by Ajigasawa town where he lived.

Then, in February 2011, he was appointed as a special

ambassador dog for World Heritage projects by the National

Federation of UNESCO Associations in Japan and helped in

fundraising for the victims of the East Japan Great Earthquake.

北国の春

　　雪道を牽く

　　　　荷馬かな

きたぐにのはる

　　ゆきみちをひく

　　　　にうまかな

季語　　春（春）

青森県・岩手県にまたがる南部地方は南部馬（なんぶうま）で有名。南部馬は、土産の馬に大形の外国馬を交配した改良種。体が大きく、性格は大人しいが、力が強いと言われる。

Kita guni no haru

yuki michi o hiku

niuma kana

The packhorse

is dragging along the snow trail

in the north country in spring

Season word: *haru* (spring; spring)

The Nanbu region, covering Aomori prefecture and Iwate prefecture, is known for the local horse breed, called the Nanbu Horse. They are sturdy and strong, but their disposition is gentle.

March

Photograph 3. Dog pilgrimage to Ise Grand Shrine, under Wikimedia Commons license, "Tokaidō Fifty-Three Stations: Yokkaichi Station, Pilgrimage Road, Oiwake, Hinaka village," circa 1840, https://commons.wikimedia.org/wiki/File:東海道五十三次_四日市_日永村追分_参宮道-Yokkaichi_MET_DP123194.jpg

土蛙

　　一雨ごとに

　　　　春来たる

つちがえる

　　ひとさめごとに

　　　　はるきたる

季語　土蛙（春）　春来たる（春）

Tsuchi gaeru

hito same goto ni

haru kitaru

The wrinkled frog knows

that each time it rains

the arrival of spring draws closer

Season words: *tsuchi gaeru* (wrinkled frog, *rana rugosa*;

spring) and *haru kitaru* (spring has come; spring)

啓蟄や

　　卵見守る

　　　赤蛙

けいちつや

　　たまごみまもる

　　　あかがえる

季語　啓蟄（春）　赤蛙（春）

赤蛙が卵の孵るのをじっと待つ様子。啓蟄とは、虫が土から出てくること。2018年の啓蟄は、日としては、3月6日で、米国のグラウンドホッグ・デイに相当。期間としては、3月6日からの3月20日までをさす。

Keichitsu ya

    tamago mi mamoru

        aka gaeru

On Keichitsu Day

    the brown frog is watching

        for her eggs to spawn

Season words: *Keichitsu* (*Keichitsu*, around March 6;
spring) and *aka gaeru* (Japanese brown frog, *rana
japonica*; spring)

In the 24-point solar terms, *Keichitsu* (*lit.*, "the wintering
insects appear from the ground") refers to the third point
among the 24, which usually begins on March 6 and lasts
until March 20. The first day of *Keichitsu* is an equivalent
of Groundhog Day.

青き踏む

　　浅黄の翅の

　　　　青き筋

あおきふむ

　　あさぎのはねの

　　　　あおきすじ

季語　青き踏む（春）

「青き踏む」は、若草の生えた春の野山のこと。「浅黄の翅」
は、羽化したばかりの紋黄蝶のことをさす。

Aoki fumu

    asagi no hane no

        aoki suji

In the spring green field

    the pale yellow wings

        show their green stripes

Season word: *aoki fumu* (spring field filled with fresh green grass; spring)

The pale yellow wings refer to the of Eastern pale clouded yellow butterfly.

お伊勢参り

　　お札をつけて

　　　歩く犬

おいせまいり

　　おふだをつけて

　　　あるくいぬ

季語　伊勢参り（春）

江戸時代の「犬の伊勢参り」の慣習。犬が伊勢参りの道中であることがわかるように、「伊勢参り」と書いたお札とお賽銭の入った袋を犬の首につけて旅に出した。わざわざ、犬を江戸から遠方の伊勢まで行かせたことは、当時、犬が大切な存在であったことを示す一例と考えられている。

O Ise mairi

    o fuda o tsuke te

        aruku inu

On the Ise Shrine pilgrimage

    the dog is walking

        wearing a prayer tag

Season word: *Ise mairi* (pilgrimage to Ise Grand Shrine; spring)

It was a custom to visit Ise Grand Shrine in spring, causing a grand migration of people, like the Islamic pilgrimage to Mecca. Japanese even sent their dogs on the pilgrimage. It took at least two weeks on foot from Edo (current Tokyo) to Ise. Local folk on the Tōkaidō Road recognized the dogs wearing the pilgrimage tag and gave them food and water on their way to Ise and back.

広重の

　　描きし犬の

　　　　伊勢参り

ひろしげの

　　えがきしいぬの

　　　　いせまいり

季語　　伊勢参り（春）

江戸時代の「犬の伊勢参り」の慣習は、歌川（安藤）広重
の版画「東海道五十三次」にも描かれていることから、庶
民の間で流行していたことがわかる。東海道五十三次の
中、四十四次の宿場、四日市の版画の中央に伊勢参りの
白い犬がいる。四日市の日永（ひなか）村・追分から、伊勢
参宮道に入るため、四日市の宿場はよく栄えたという。

Hiroshige no

    egaki shi inu no

        Ise mairi

Hiroshige drew

    the scene of the dog pilgrimage

        to Ise Grand Shrine

Season word: *Ise mairi* (pilgrimage to Ise Grand Shrine; spring)

The renowned woodblock print painter, Utagawa (Andō) Hiroshige (1797–1858), drew the scene of the dog pilgrimage to Ise Grand Shrine as one of his famous Scenes of the Fifty-Three Stations of the Tōkaidō. A white pilgrimage dog is depicted for Station 44: Yokkaichi. At Oiwake, Hinaka village, in Yokkaichi, pilgrims switched to the Ise Pilgrimage Road from the Tōkaidō Road.

京の梅

　　　空つぽの檻を

　　　　漂ひて

きょうのうめ

　　　からっぽのおりを

　　　　ただよいて

季語　　梅（春）

太平洋戦争中の1943年8月、日本政府は戦時危険動物
処分政策を全国の動物園に発令した。京都市立動物園
は、東京の上野恩賜動物園や大阪市立動物園のように直
ちに施行しなかったが、1944年3月、遂に施行を余儀なく
させられ、クマやトラなど、計9種・14頭の動物を処分（射
殺・絞殺・薬殺）した。

Kyō no ume

    karappo no ori o

        tadayoi te

The plum blossoms in Kyoto

    their scent drifts

        into the empty cages

Season word: *ume* (plum blossoms; spring)

In August 1943 during World War II, the Japanese government issued the disposal order for dangerous animals at zoos nationwide. The Kyoto City Zoo in Kyoto prefecture resisted the order until March 1944, when it destroyed a total of 14 animals of 9 species, including bears and tigers. For details, please see *Japanese Wartime Zoo Policy: The Silent Victims of World War II* (2010).

白浜や

　　風に微睡む

　　　　桜貝

しらはまや

　　かぜにまどろむ

　　　　さくらがい

季語　桜貝（春）

和歌山県白浜町は、美しい砂浜と温泉で有名。

Shirahama ya

    kaze ni madoromu

        sakura gai

In Shirahama

    the sakura shellfish is taking a nap

        in the gentle sea wind

Season word: *sakura gai* (*lit.*, "cherry blossom seashell,"

nitidotellina nitidua; spring)

Shirahama, Wakayama prefecture, is famous for its beautiful white beach and hot springs. It is a popular tourist resort, south of Osaka.

桜貝

　　空と海とに

　　　　磨かれて

さくらがい

　　そらとうみとに

　　　　みがかれて

季語　桜貝（春）

Sakura gai

    sora to umi toni

        migakare te

The sakura shellfish

    is being polished

        by the sky and the sea

Season word: *sakura gai* (*lit.*, "cherry blossom seashell," *nitidotellina nitidua*; spring)

The *sakura gai* is a pretty pink seashell (*rosa sakuragai*, a species of tellin).

春鰯

　　銀鱗の群

　　　光る海

はるいわし

　　ぎんりんのむれ

　　　ひかるうみ

季語　春鰯（春）

鰯は、本来、秋の季語であるが、日本海沿岸の鰯漁は春に行われるので、春鰯と呼ばれる。

Haru iwashi

ginrin no mure

hikaru umi

The silver scales

of the school of spring sardines

are shining in the sea

Season word: *haru iwashi* (spring sardines; spring)

"Sardine" itself is a season word of autumn, but the

sardines are caught in the spring on the coast of the Sea of

Japan and are called "spring sardines."

鯨法会

　　寺の鐘鳴り

　　　海の鳴る

くじらほうえ

　　てらのかねなり

　　　うみのなる

季語　　鯨法会（春）

江戸時代から明治時代初期まで、古式捕鯨の行なわれて

いた山口県長門市の幾つかの寺では、現在も、毎年3月

に鯨法会（回向）を行なう。始まりの合図に浜の寺が鐘を

鳴らす。山口県仙崎村（現在、長門市）生まれの金子み

すゞ（1903年−1930年）の詩にも謳われている。

Kujira hōe

    tera no kane nari

      umi no naru

The memorial service for whales

    the sea is resounding

      with the bell of the temple

Season word: *kujira hōe* (memorial service for whales; spring)

Fishing villages in Japan, including Nagato, Yamaguchi prefecture, which had engaged in classical whaling, have conducted memorial services for whales every year to this day, even after they had stopped whaling more than a hundred years ago. The female poet in Senzaki (current Nagato), Kaneko Misuzu (1903–1930), wrote a poignant poem about this.

April

Photograph 4. Bronze Statue of Saigō Takamori with Satsuma-inu Tsun, Ueno Park, Tokyo, under Creative Commons license, "Saigō Takamori," August 23, 2004, https://ccsearch.creativecommons.org/?search=saigo+taka mori

岐阜蝶や

　　千年前の

　　　　舞踊る

ぎふちょうや

　　せんねんまえの

　　　　まいおどる

季語　　岐阜蝶（春）

ギフチョウの成虫は、早春に羽化し、晩春に消えることから、

「春の女神」と呼ばれる。近年、里山の開発などにより、個

体数の減少が著しい。群馬県や新潟県では、県の天然記

念物に指定されている。環境省により、絶滅危惧 II 類の

指定を受け、さらに、国際自然保護連合からは、レッドリス

トの準絶滅危惧の指定を受けている。

Gifu chō ya

    sen'nen mae no

        mai odoru

The Japanese luehdorfia butterfly

    is dancing the dance

        from a thousand years ago

Season word: *gifu chō* (Japanese luehdorfia butterfly; spring)

The Japanese luehdorfia butterfly appears early in spring and perishes in late spring; hence it is referred to as "spring ephemeral" or "spring goddess." The population of this species has drastically decreased as its habitats have been destroyed and it is listed as endangered.

鶯の

　　やうなさへづり

　　　異国の空よ

うぐいすの

　　ようなさえずり

　　　いこくのそらよ

季語　鶯（春）

Uguisu no

    yōna saezuri

        ikoku no sora yo

Listening to the American warbler

    one thinks of the homeland

        where the Japanese bush warbler sings

Season word: *uguisu* (Japanese bush warbler; spring)

The Japanese bush warbler is known for its beautiful calls

and is prized in Japan. It is appreciated in paintings, poems,

and other forms of Japanese art and literature.

ハチ公や

　　初のお花見

　　　　空の笑む

ハチこうや

　　はつのおはなみ

　　　　そらのえむ

季語　　花見（桜の花見、詩歌では花は桜をさす、春）

渋谷のハチ公の飼い主、上野英三郎は、毎年、大学の同僚の教授や学生を招いて、自宅の庭で盛大な花見の宴を催した。1924年4月、まだ子犬であったハチは、招待客を迎えるために、花見の前日に綺麗に身体を洗ってもらった。それはハチの初めてのお風呂であった。そして、この花見は、ハチの最初で最後の花見となった。上野は翌年5月に亡くなる。

Hachi kō ya

    hatsu no o hanami

        sora no emu

Hachi-kō

    had his first cherry blossom viewing

        and the sky smiled

Season word: *hana-mi* (cherry blossom viewing; spring)

Hachi's owner, Ueno Hidesaburō, held a splendid cherry

blossom viewing party in his garden every year, inviting his

colleagues and students at the Tokyo Imperial University

Agricultural College. The one in April 1924 was Hachi's

first such party and became his last. Ueno fell ill and died

in May 1925.

花の宴

　　子犬の座る

　　　緋毛氈

はなのえん

　　こいぬのすわる

　　　ひもうせん

季語　花の宴（春）

花の宴は、桜の花見の宴のこと。

Hana no en

    ko inu no suwaru

        hi mōsen

At the cherry blossom viewing party

    a puppy sits

        on the red carpet primly

Season word: *hana no en* (cherry blossom viewing party; spring)

In haiku, hana refers to cherry blossoms.

上野の春

　　西郷どんを

　　　　仰ぐハチ

うえののはる

　　さいごうどんを

　　　　あおぐハチ

季語　　春（春）

ハチは、実際に上野公園で薩摩犬ツン（メス）を連れた西
郷隆盛（1828年–1877年）の銅像（高村光雲作）を見て
いる。渋谷の「忠犬ハチ公像」を作った安藤照（1892年
–1945年）は、西郷の郷里の鹿児島に軍服を着た西郷隆
盛像を新たに製作した。

Ueno no haru

Saigō don o

aogu Hachi

At Ueno Park in spring

Hachi looked up

at the Statue of Saigō Takamori

Season word: *haru* (spring; spring)

The leader of the Meiji Restoration, Saigō Takamori

(1828–1870), loved dogs and his bronze statue at Ueno

Park, made by Takamura Kōun, is accompanied by a statue

of a female Satsuma-inu Tsun. Andō Teru (1892–1945),

who made the original bronze statue of Hachi-kō, created

another magnificent statue of Saigō for his hometown,

Kagoshima.

ハチ公や

　　弾丸（たま）と変はりて

　　　散る桜

ハチこうや

　　たまとかわりて

　　　ちるさくら

季語　桜（春）

渋谷の「忠犬ハチ公像」は、戦時金属供出運動が厳しくな
る中、「戦争が終わるまで倉庫に保管しておく」という鉄道
省との合意にもかかわらず、1944年に取り外され、その後、
溶解された。実際には、武器ではなく、省線（国鉄の前身）
の機関車の一部となり、東海道本線を走った。

Hachi kō ya

    tama to kawari te

        chiru sakura

Hachi-kō

    turned into bullets

        and fell like the cherry blossom petals

Season word: *sakura* (cherry blossoms; spring)

This is an image of the fate of the Hachi-kō Bronze Statue

at Shibuya Station in Tokyo. During the wartime metal

recycling by the Japanese government, the Hachi-kō

Bronze Statue was taken down in 1944 and melted down in

1945, despite the agreement to keep it in a storage until the

war was over. In reality, it was turned into part of an

engine for the Japanese Government Railways.

栗林の

　　雌豹射たれ

　　　　花の泣く

りつりんの

　　めすひょううたれ

　　　　はなのなく

季語　　花(桜、春)

香川県高松市の栗林公園動物園(1930年1月開園、20

04年3月閉鎖)では、ライオン、ハイエナ、クマなどを飼育

しており、戦時危険動物処分を施行したが、公式記録は

残っていない。新聞記事には、1944年4月11日、雌豹が

檻から逃げ、地元の猟友会会員により射殺されたとある。

Ritsurin no

    mesu hyō utare

        hana no naku

The female leopard

    at Ritsurin Park was shot

        and the cherry blossoms wept

Season word: *hana* (cherry blossoms; spring)

Ritsurin Park in Takamatsu, Kagawa prefecture, is one of

the most venerable and praised gardens in Japan. Per the

wartime government disposal order of dangerous animals,

the Ritsurin Park Zoo destroyed its animals, but no official

record was preserved. The newspaper merely reported on

April 11, 1944 that a female leopard had escaped from the

zoo and was shot by a local hunting club member.

津軽富士

　　雪解けわさおの

　　　心溶け

つがるふじ

　　ゆきとけわさおの

　　　こころとけ

季語　雪解ける（春）

青森県弘前市および西津軽郡鰺ヶ沢町（わさおの住む）
に位置する岩木山（成層火山）は、その美しい姿から、「津
軽富士」と呼ばれ、地元住民の間で親しまれてきた。

Tsugaru Fuji

> yuki toke Wasao no

> kokoro toke

Mt. Tsugaru Fuji

> the snow on the mountain melts

> and melts the heart of Wasao

Season word: *yuki tokeru* (snow melts; spring)
Wasao lives in Ajigasawa town, Nishi–Tsugaru county,
Aomori prefecture, where the stratovolcano, Mt. Iwaki,
soars on the border of Ajigasawa and Hirosaki. Its graceful
shape resembles Mt. Fuji; hence it is generally known as
Mt. Tsugaru Fuji.

津軽桜

　　わさおの白毛

　　　くすぐりて

つがるざくら

　　わさおのしろげ

　　　くすぐりて

季語　津軽桜（春）

わさおは、白の長毛の秋田犬である。桜前線の北上に伴い、北国の津軽地方にも桜の季節が訪れる。弘前公園などの地元の花の名所は、全国からの観光客で賑わう。

Tsugaru zakura

Wasao no shiro ge

kusuguri te

Tsugaru cherry blossoms

their petals are tickling

the white coat of Wasao

Season word: *sakura* (cherry blossoms; spring)

Tsugaru cherry trees in the northern region are late
bloomers, and tourists flock to see the blossoms at Hirosaki
Castle Park, after cherry blossoms in other parts of Japan
have gone. Wasao is a long-haired Akita-inu.

花吹雪

　　「花咲か爺」の

　　　犬と臼

はなふぶき

　　はなさかじじいの

　　　いぬとうす

季語　花吹雪(春)

昔話、「花咲か爺」の逸話。

Hana fubuki

Hana saka jijii no

inu to usu

The cherry blossom shower

is falling on the dog and the wooden mortar

in the story of Old Man Cherry Blossoms

Season word: *hana fubuki* (*lit.*, "cherry blossom shower,"

falling cherry blossoms; spring)

This refers to the Japanese folk tale, *Hanasaka jijii* (Old

Man Cherry Blossoms), in which a kind old man and his

dog, killed by a wicked neighbor, resuscitated a dead

cherry tree.

May

Photograph 5. Wasao and rapeseed flowers, May 7, 2018,

© wasao project, Wasao's Facebook page,

https://www.facebook.com/wasao.official

菜の花や

　　わさおの頬を

　　　　そっと撫で

なのはなや

　　わさおのほほを

　　　　そっとなで

季語　菜の花（春）

春の訪れの遅い津軽地方では、菜の花は5月に咲く。

Nano hana ya

   Wasao no hoho o

      sotto nade

The rapeseed flowers

   gently touch

      the cheeks of Wasao

Season word: *nano hana* (rapeseed flowers; spring)

Spring comes late in the Tsugaru region, and rapeseed blooms in early May, not in April.

雛孵る

　　世の煩ひを

　　　　暫し忘るる

ひなかえる

　　よのわずらいを

　　　　しばしわするる

季語　　雛孵る（春）

湖で、鴨や雁などの水鳥の雛を観ていると、人の世の煩わ

しさを一時忘れ、自然に感謝する気持ちに満たされる。

Hina kaeru

    yo no wazurai o

        shibashi wasururu

The chicks have hatched

    and one forgets the worries of daily life

        for the moment

Season word: *hina kaeru* (chicks have hatched; spring)

木曽馬や

　　産声響く

　　　春の空

きそうまや

　　うぶごえひびく

　　　はるのそら

季語　　春の空（春）

2018年5月、6年振りに木曽馬の赤ちゃんが誕生した。母馬は、14歳の藤富（ふじとみ）。ずんぐりした胴体から伸びるたくましい脚、人懐っこそうな優しい眼が印象的。木曽馬は、日清戦争以降、体が小さいことから軍馬に向かないとされ、絶滅寸前となる。太平洋戦争後、保護活動が始まり（木曽馬保存会）、現在は全国で約140頭が飼育されている。

Kiso uma ya

    ubu goe hibiku

        haru no sora

The Kiso Horse

    the first neighing of the foal

        is reverberating in the spring sky

Season word: *haru no sora* (spring sky; spring)

In May 2018, a foal was born to a Kiso Horse (the indigenous

breed in Nagano prefecture) for the first time in six years. The

mother was the 14-year old Fujitomi. After the Sino-Japanese

War (1894–1895), this breed was considered unfit as war horses

(due to its small size) and were brought to the blink of extinction.

After the end of the Asia–Pacific War in 1945, a rehabilitation

effort for the breed began and the number has recovered to about

140 today.

伊豆の園

　　菖蒲湯に酔ふ

　　　　カピバラ親子

いずのその

　　しょうぶゆによう

　　　　カピバラおやこ

季語　　菖蒲湯（夏）　　俳句では、5月5日から夏となる。

「子供の日」に、子供の健康を祈り、厄除けに薬用成分の

ある菖蒲湯に入れる習慣。菖蒲湯は強い芳香があり、子

供には酔うほど。静岡県伊東市の「伊豆シャボテン動物公

園」では、カピバラ親子を露天風呂の菖蒲湯に入れる。

Izu no sono

shōbu yu ni you

kapibara oyako

In Izu Park Zoo

the capybara family are taking an iris bath

and are drunk

Season word: *shōbu yu* (iris bath; summer) For haiku,

summer begins on May 5.

It is a tradition to have children take bath with iris leaves on

May 5, the Day of Children, in Japan, wishing for their

health. The iris leaves have medicinal effects. Their strong

scent makes one feel like being drunk. Izu Park Zoo in Itō,

Shizuoka prefecture, gives its capybara family an iris bath.

燕の子

　　口を開ければ

　　　　燕子花

つばめのこ

　　くちをあければ

　　　　かきつばた

季語　燕の子（夏）　燕子花（夏）

燕の子の口を開いた様子は、まさに、燕子花である。

Tsubame no ko

kuchi o akereba

kaki tsubata

The barn swallow chicks

open their mouths wide

that look like iris flowers

Season words: *tsubame no ko* (barn swallow chicks;

summer) and *kaki tsubata* (iris; summer)

One of the names for iris in Chinese characters literally

means "the swallow chick flower.

長良川

　　烏帽子操る

　　　　鵜の浮かぶ

ながらがわ

　　えぼしあやつる

　　　　うのうかぶ

季語　　鵜（川鵜、夏）

1300年以上の歴史を持つ岐阜県長良川鵜飼が5月11日開幕した。風折烏帽子（かざおりえぼし）を被った鵜匠の操る川鵜がアユを捕らえる。

Nagara gawa

    eboshi ayatsuru

        u no ukabu

At Nagara River

    the eboshi hats are handling

        the floating cormorants

Season word: *u* (great cormorant; summer)

The *ukai* (*lit.*, "raising cormorants") on Nagara River, Gifu

prefecture, is a 1,300-year old tradition, in which the *ukai*

masters train great cormorants to catch *ayu* (sweetfish).

The season runs from May 11 to October 15. The *eboshi* is

the traditional formal headwear worn by court nobles.

Because of their special skills and stature, the *ukai* masters

were allowed to wear this hat.

鵜飼舟

　　かがり火に潜る

　　　百羽の鵜

うかいぶね

　　かがりびにもぐる

　　　ひゃくわのう

季語　　鵜飼舟（夏）　鵜（夏）

鵜飼舟のかがり火が川面を照らす中、鵜匠と川鵜が絶妙のコラボを披露。チャールズ・チャップリン（1889年–1977年）は、1936年に来日した際に長良川鵜飼を観て感動し、1961年に再来日した際にも長良川鵜飼を鑑賞した。

Ukai bune

    kagaribi ni moguru

        hyakuwa no u

From the fishing boats

    a hundred cormorants

        are diving onto the fishing fire

Season words: *ukai bune* (cormorant fishing boat; summer)

and *u* (great cormorant; summer)

The *ukai* masters release great cormorants with a rope tied

to them into Nagara River, in which the fishing fire is

reflected. Charles Chaplin was taken by the art of

cormorant fishing during his visit to Japan in 1936 and saw

the performance again during his visit to Japan in 1961.

夏の大掃除

　　亡父の布団に

　　　犬の哭く

なつのおおそうじ

　　ぼうふのふとんに

　　　いぬのなく

季語　　夏の大掃除（夏）

昔、流行病を防ぐために梅雨の前に大掃除をした慣習。
夏の大掃除で亡父の布団を処理していた時に、飼い犬が
亡父の匂いを嗅ぎつけ、亡父を思い出して鳴きわめいたと
いう実話より。渋谷のハチ公にもよく似たことが起こった。

Natsu no ō sōji

bōfu no futon ni

inu no naku

In the summer cleaning

the dog smells the futon

of the dead owner and cries

Season word: *natsu no ō-sōji* (the summer cleaning of the

house; summer)

This describes a scene of the summer cleaning, in which a

dog sniffed out an old futon mattress that had been kept in a

closet, and the dog suddenly remembered his dead owner.

A similar thing happened to Hachi-kō, when his owner

Ueno Hidesaburō died in May 1925.

青嵐

　　霊柩車追ふ

　　　犬を追ふ

あおあらし

　　れいきゅうしゃおう

　　　いぬをおう

季語　青嵐（夏）

1925年5月21日にハチ公の飼い主、上野英三郎は死去
したが、お通夜の最中、ハチ公は座敷に上がり込み、棺の
下に潜り込んで離れようとしなかった。その姿が家人の涙
を誘ったという。

Ao arashi

   reikyūsha ou

      inu o ou

The summer green wind

   is chasing the dog

      who is chasing the hearse that carries his

   dead owner

Season word: *ao arashi* (summer wind; summer)

This describes an image of Hachi-kō at the funeral of his

owner, Ueno Hidesaburō, in May 1925. Hachi-kō snuck

into the living room where Ueno's wake was conducted.

He lay down under Ueno's coffin and refused to move,

making the attendants shed tears in sympathy.

花菖蒲

　　　小象のはな子

　　　　大往生

はなしょうぶ

　　　こぞうのはなこ

　　　　だいおうじょう

季語　　花菖蒲（夏）

戦時危険動物処分政策により上野恩賜動物園の象3頭は餓死

させられた。戦後、1949年、同園はタイより小さい象を輸入し、

死んだ花子にちなんで、はな子と名付け大歓迎した。象の飼育

員であった渋谷信吉は、この人間の身勝手に失望した。その後、

はな子は、井の頭自然文化園に移され、市民の虐待を受ける。

飼育員山川清蔵の献身的な世話の結果、はな子は健康を回復

し最長寿の象となった（1947年春–2016年5月26日）。

Hana shōbu

   kozō no Hanako

    daiōjō

The iris grieves

   at the death of the Asian elephant

    Hanako

Season word: *hana shōbu* (iris; summer)

An Asian elephant Gacha (1947–May 25, 2016) was brought

from Thailand in 1949, after all the elephants at Ueno Zoo in

Tokyo had been destroyed in the Wartime Disposal of

Dangerous Animals order. She was named Hanako after one of

the destroyed elephants. The zookeeper Shibuya Shinkichi was

disgusted with the human selfishness. Hanako was transferred to

Inokashira Park Zoo and was abused by citizens there. The

zookeeper Yamakawa Seizō's devoted care saved Hanako, who

lived to be one of the oldest elephants in Japan.

June

Photograph 6. Canada geese and goslings crossing the street by a lake, taken by the author

朝凪や

　　無言歌を聞く

　　　　鳥の鳴く

あさなぎや

　　むごんかをきく

　　　　とりのなく

季語　朝凪（夏）

Asa nagi ya

    mugonka o kiku

        tori no naku

In the morning calm of the sea

    the bird listens to the song without words of the sea

        and sings along quietly

Season word: *asa nagi* (morning calm of the sea; summer)

紫陽花や

　　夢を走らせ

　　　象列車

あじさいや

　　ゆめをはしらせ

　　　ぞうれっしゃ

季語　　紫陽花（夏）

1949年6月18日、最初の「象列車」が東京から名古屋に走った。戦後、名古屋市立東山動物園は、北王英一園長の抵抗の結果、日本で象（二頭）が生き残った唯一の動物園となった。しかし、北王は、象を見たいという子供達のために一頭の象を上野恩賜動物園に移すという依頼を断った。仲間の他の二頭が栄養失調で死んでいく中、戦争を生き延びた二頭の象を引き離すことはできなかった。子供達を名古屋に連れて来るという北王の叡智と尽力により編成されたのが「象列車」であった。

Ajisai ya

    yume o hashira se

      zōressha

The hydrangea

    sends off the Elephant Train

      carrying the dreams of children

Season word: *ajisai* (hydrangea; summer)

On June 18, 1949, the first Elephant Train ran to Nagoya from

Tokyo. The train carried children, not elephants. After World

War II, only two elephants lived in Japan, at Higashiyama Zoo in

Nagoya (all of the others had been destroyed). Zoo director

Kitaō Hideichi declined the request of Ueno Zoo in Tokyo to

send one of the two elephants to Ueno Zoo, because the two

elephants had survived the war together and were inseperable

Instead, Kitaō came up with the idea to bring children to Nagoya

to see the elephants. This was the origin of the Elephant Train.

蛇の目傘

　　迷ひ子猫の

　　　　雨宿り

じゃのめがさ

　　まよいごねこの

　　　　あまやどり

季語　　雨宿り（夏）

Janome gasa

> mayoigo neko no

> > ama yadori

Under the janome umbrella

> the lost kitten

> > is taking shelter from the rain

Season word: *ama yadoi* (taking shelter from the rain;
summer)

The *janome gasa* is a large umbrella made of waxed paper
with a bull's eye design.

交通止め

　　軽鴨親子の

　　　　お引越し

こうつうどめ

　　かるがもおやこの

　　　　おひっこし

季語　　軽鴨（夏）

毎年恒例となった、軽鴨の親鳥が育った雛を巣から皇居
の外堀や京都の鴨川へ引越しさせる年中行事。米国でも
カナダ雁の親子が道路を横断して、よく車を止める。

Kōtsū dome

karugamo oyako no

o hikkoshi

The traffic stopped

and the spot-billed duck family

is moving

Season word: *karu gamo* (Asian spot-billed duck; summer)

It has become an annual event to stop the traffic in front of

the Imperial Palace outer moat in Tokyo, so that the spot-

billed duck family can cross the busy road safely to the

moat from the pond on the other side of the road, where the

ducklings were hatched. It is the March of Ducks.

青き空

　　軽鴨一家

　　　　草を食む

あおきそら

　　かるがもいっか

　　　　くさをはむ

季語　　軽鴨（夏）

Aoki sora

karugamo ikka

kusa o hamu

Under the blue sky

the spot-billed duck family

is grazing

Season word: *karu gamo* (Asian spot-billed duck; summer)

水馬

　　湖畔の宿の

　　　　渡し守

あめんぼう

　　こはんのやどの

　　　　わたしもり

季語　水馬（あめんぼう、夏）

水馬（あめんぼう）は、ミズスマシ（水澄し）の別名。

Amenbō

kohan no yado no

watashi mori

The water strider

sails like the ferryman

of the inn by the lake

Season word: *amenbō* (water strider, *gerridae*; summer)

初蛍

　　一夜の星と

　　　　なりにけり

はつほたる

　　ひとよのほしと

　　　　なりにけり

季語　初蛍（夏）

Hatsu hotaru

hitoyo no hoshi to

nari ni keri

The first firefly came

and became a star

for the night

Season word: *hatsu hotaru* (first firefly of the season;

summer)

夏蛍

　　魔法の森の

　　　　道案内

なつほたる

　　まほうのもりの

　　　　みちあない

季語　夏蛍（夏）

Natsu hotaru

   mahō no mori no

      michi anai

The summer firefly

   is guiding one

      to the enchanted wood

Season word: *natsu hotaru* (summer firefly; summer)

森深し

　　薔薇の香に棲む

　　　　母仔鹿

もりふかし

　　ばらのかにすむ

　　　　ははこじか

季語　　薔薇（夏）

Mori fukashi

bara no ka ni sumu

hahako jika

Deep in the wood

the doe and her fawns

live in the scent of roses

Season word: *bara* (rose; summer)

森の笑む

　　鹿の子双子の

　　　　隠れんぼ

もりのえむ

　　かのこふたごの

　　　　かくれんぼ

季語　鹿の子（夏）

Mori no emu

   kanoko futago no

      kakurenbo

The twin fawns

   are playing hide and seek

      and the wood smiles

Season word: *kanoko* (fawn; summer)

July

Photograph 7. Turtles sunbathing, taken by the author

夏立ちぬ

　　木曽の嘶

　　　木霊して

なつたちぬ

　　きそのいななき

　　　こだまして

季語　夏立ちぬ（夏）

長野県木曽地方は、本州で唯一の日本在来種の馬である木曽馬の産地。他の日本の在来種の馬と同様、絶滅危惧種である。2018年5月に14歳の木曽馬、藤富（ふじとみ）の産んだ仔馬が元気に育っている様子が微笑ましい。

Natsu tachi nu

Kiso no inanaki

kodama shite

Summer has come

and the neighing of the horse

is echoing in the sky in Kiso

Season word: *natsu tachinu* (summer has come; summer)

The Kiso Horse foal born to the 14-year-old Fujitomi in

May 2018 has grown well. Like most other indigenous

horse breeds of Japan, the Kiso Horse is critically

endangered.

せせらぎに

　　トレモロ添へる

　　　　河鹿かな

せせらぎに

　　トレモロそえる

　　　　かじかかな

季語　河鹿（カジカガエル、夏）

河鹿（カジカガエル）は、その美しい鳴き声が夏の山地の
風物詩として知られる。鳴き声が雄鹿に似ていることから、
河鹿と呼ばれている。

Seseragi ni

   toremoro soeru

      kajika kana

The sound of the brook

   is accompanied by the tremolo

      of the kajika frog

Season word: *kajika* (kajika frog, *buergeria buergeri*;

summer)

Kajika literally means "river deer." The beautiful calls of

kajika frog sound like a male deer; hence the name.

夏燕

　　　　歌の翼と

　　　　　　白き雲

なつつばめ

　　　うたのつばさと

　　　　　　しろきくも

季語　　夏燕（夏）

燕自体は、春の季語であるが、夏燕は夏の季語となる。

Natsu tsubame

uta no tsubasa to

shiroki kumo

The summer swallow

is singing spreading its wings

in the white clouds

Season word: *natsu tsubame* (summer swallow; summer)

The swallow itself is a season word of spring, whereas the summer swallow signifies summer.

海開き

　　砂に身隠す

　　　桜貝

うみびらき

　　すなにみかくす

　　　さくらがい

季語　海開き（夏）

桜貝は、春の季語であるが、この句では季語として使われ
ていない（虚偽の季語）。

Umi biraki

    suna ni mikakusu

        sakura gai

At the beach opening

    the pink seashell

        hides in the sand

Season word: *umi biraki* (beach opening; summer)

Sakura gai (pink seashell, *nitidotellina nitidua*) is a season

word of spring; however, in this haiku, it is not used as a

season word. In haiku, this is referred to as a "false season

word."

赤珊瑚

　　月の雫と

　　　　眠りたり

あかさんご

　　つきのしずくと

　　　　ねむりたり

季語　月の雫（真珠、夏）

月の雫は、真珠の別名。

6月1日は、「真珠の日」、7月11日は「真珠記念日」。

Aka sango

    tsuki no shizuku to

        nemuri tari

The red coral

    is slumbering

        with the "moon drops"

Season word: *tsuki no shizuku* ("moon drops" refers to

pearls; summer)

"Moon drops" is a euphemism for pearls.

June 1 is the Day of Pearls and July 11 is the Day to

Commemorate Pearls in Japan.

海亀や

　　　産卵の涙

　　　　月の看る

うみがめや

　　　さんらんのなみだ

　　　　つきのみる

季語　海亀（夏）

成長した海亀は、20年後自分の生まれた浜に戻って産卵
する。産卵時に涙を流すと言われる。この「涙」は、実際は、
体内の塩分を排出・調整するために流されているものであ
るが、産卵の苦痛には変わりないであろう。

Umi game ya

    sanran no namida

        tsuki no miru

The sea turtle

    is shedding tears

        as she lays her eggs under the moon

Season word: *umi game* (sea turtle; summer)

Mature (about 20 years old) sea turtles return to the beach where they hatched in order to lay eggs. It has been said that they shed tears as they lay eggs. They are actually extracting the extra salt from the "salt glands" behind their eyes in order to maintain the salt balance in their bodies. Nonetheless, labor is labor.

満月や

　　子亀導き

　　　大海原へ

まんげつや

　　こがめみちびき

　　　おおうなばらへ

季語　　子亀（夏）

海亀の卵は産卵から2カ月後、満月の夜に孵化し、海に旅立つと言われる。そして20年後に産まれた浜に戻ってきて産卵する。そして、この悠久の自然のサイクルが繰り返される。

Man getsu ya

    ko game michibiki

      ō una bara e

The full moon

    is guiding the sea turtle hatchlings

      to the great ocean

Season word: *umi game no ko* (sea turtle hatchlings; summer)

Sea turtle eggs hatch on the night of the full moon, two months after they were laid, and the hatchings immediately head to the ocean. Twenty years later, mature sea turtles return to the beach where they hatched and lay eggs.

親亀と

　　子亀寄り添ひ

　　　　甲羅干し

おやがめと

　　こがめよりそい

　　　　こうらぼし

季語　　子亀（夏）

Oya game to

    ko kame yori soi

        kōra boshi

The mother turtle

    and her baby turtles

        are sunbathing side by side

Season word: *ko game* (baby turtle; summer)

天道虫

　　ポルカ・ドットに

　　　葉をカット

てんとうむし

　　ポルカ・ドットに

　　　はをカット

季語　天道虫（夏）

Tentō mushi

poruka dotto ni

ha o katto

The ladybug

is eating the leaf

making it look like polka dots

Season word: *tentō mushi* (ladybug; summer)

鴉啼く

　　麦藁帽子の

　　　　ファン・ゴッホ

からすなく

　　むぎわらぼうしの

　　　　ファン・ゴッホ

季語　　麦藁帽子（夏）

フィンセント・ファン・ゴッホ（1853年–1890年）のオマージュ。麦藁帽子を被った自画像を描き、さらに、最期の油彩画、「カラスのいる麦畑」には、無数のカラスを描いた。ファン・ゴッホの命日は、7月29日である。俳句では、カラスは、鳥ではなく鴉と表記する。

Karasu naku

   mugi wara bōshi no

      fan Gohho

The crow cries

   watching the straw hat

      of van Gogh

Season word: *mugi wara bōshi* (straw hat; summer)

This is a homage to Vincent van Gogh (1853–1890), who

died on July 29. His oil paintings include "Self-Portrait

with Straw Hat" (1887) and "Wheatfield with Crows"

(1890).

August

Photograph 8. Chinese tropical fritillary butterfly, Komaki

Citizens' Forest for Four Seasons, Komaki, Aichi

prefecture, August 2010, taken by the author

山開き

　　揚羽の休む

　　　バンガロー

やまびらき

　　あげはのやすむ

　　　バンガロー

季語　山開き（夏）　揚羽（揚羽蝶、夏）

Yama biraki

   ageha no yasumu

      bangarō

The opening of the mountaineering season

   finds the swallowtail butterfly

      resting in the mountain hut

Season words: *yama biraki* (opening of the mountaineering

season; summer) and *ageha* (swallowtail butterfly;

summer)

糸蜻蛉

　　翅をすぼめて

　　　風の止む

いととんぼ

　　はねをすぼめて

　　　かぜのやむ

季語　　糸蜻蛉（夏）

蜻蛉が水平に翅を広げて止まるのに対し、糸蜻蛉は、翅
を閉じて止まる。夏の水辺に棲息し、よく翅を休めると言わ
れる。

Ito tonbo

　　hane o subome te

　　　　kaze no yamu

The damselfly

　　closed its wings to rest

　　　　and the wind stops

Season word: *ito tonbo* (damselfly; summer)

The dragonfly spreads its wings horizontally when it lands

on grass. By contrast, the damselfly closes and erects its

wings when it lands on grass, often by a river, and rests.

朝蜘蛛や

　　遠き方より

　　　　友来たり

あさぐもや

　　とおきかたより

　　　　ともきたり

季語　　朝蜘蛛（夏）

朝に蜘蛛を見るとその日に良い事が起こるので、朝蜘蛛を
殺してはいけないという言い伝え。

Asa gumo ya

    tōki kata yori

        tomo kitari

The morning spider

    has brought the friend

        from far away

Season word: *kumo* (spider; summer)

A saying in Japan goes that if one finds a spider in the morning, it brings an old friend or good luck and therefore one should not kill it.

夏蜘蛛や

　　シャーロット・ウェブの

　　　命乞ひ

なつぐもや

　　シャーロット・ウェブの

　　　いのちごい

季語　　夏蜘蛛（夏）

E. B. ホワイト作の児童文学作品、『シャーロットのおくりも
の』（原題は「シャーロットの蜘蛛の巣」、1952年）に寄せ
て。

Natsu gumo ya

    Shārotto webu no

        inochi goi

The summer spider

    Charlotte's Web

        is trying to save the life of her friend

Season word: *natsu gumo* (summer spider; summer)

This is based on *Charlotte's Web* (1952) by E. B. White, in which Charlotte's web saved the life of her barn friend, Wilbur, the Pig.

馬冷やす

　　優しき眼の

　　　　青き空

うまひやす

　　やさしきまなこの

　　　　あおきそら

季語　馬冷やす（夏）

大きな馬の目に青空が映っている様子。
昔、農夫は、使役馬を川や湖で洗って冷やしてやってい
た。

Uma hiyasu

    yasashiki manako no

      aoki sora

The horse having been cooled off in the river

    its gentle eye has the reflection

      of the blue sky

Season word: *uma hiyasu* (to have a horse cool off in the water; summer)

In traditional rural communities, farmers washed their workhorses with cool water by a river or a lake after the day's work during the summer.

白兎

　　蒲の穂綿に

　　　癒されし

しろうさぎ

　　がまのほわたに

　　　いやされし

季語　　蒲の穂綿（夏）

出雲神話の「因幡の白兎」より。兎は冬の季語であるが、これは夏の逸話であると考えられる。大国主命が砂浜で白兎につけるようにと教えた蒲の穂綿（雌花の熟したもの）の先には、蒲黄（ほおう、雄花の花粉、傷薬としての効能あり）がある。この花粉は夏に飛び散ってしまう。

Shiro usagi

gama no ho wata ni

iyasare shi

The white hare

was healed

by the cattail fluff

Season word: *gama no ho-wata* (cattail fluff; summer)

This refers to the story called "White Hare of Inaba" in Izumo

Mythology. The hare is a season word of winter, but this

episode took place in summer. The Ōkuni-nushi God told the

crying hare to cover its skinned body with the cattail cotton

(white pistillate flowers) to heal its body. Actually, the cattail

has yellow staminate flowers at the tip, which has a medicinal

effect. The flowers fly away by the end of summer.

何想ひ

　　海原超ゆる

　　　　夏の蝶

なにおもい

　　うなばらこゆる

　　　　なつのちょう

季語　　夏の蝶（夏）

Nani omoi

    una bara koyuru

        natsu no chō

One wonders

    what the summer butterfly is thinking

        as it crosses the great ocean

Season word: *natsu no chō* (summer butterfly; summer)

長春の夏

　　アムール・タイガー

　　　ピノの死す

ちょうしゅんのなつ

　　アムール・タイガー

　　　ピノのしす

季語　　夏（夏）

満州重工業開発社総裁高碕達之助（1885年–1964年）は動物好きで、満州国の首都新京（長春）動物園設営に多大な私財を費やし、激務の合間を縫って動物園に行った。一番のお気に入りは、アムール・タイガーのピノ。平気でピノの檻に入り、ピノを撫でた。1945年8月9日未明、ソ連軍が満州に侵攻すると、同動物園は、日本政府の方針に従い危険動物を薬殺した。その頃、高碕は在留邦人の安全確保のために奔走し、過労と日射病から意識不明に陥った。意識が戻り、中俣充志（みつし）同園園長に最初に聞いたことは、「ピノはどうしているか」、「ピノは大丈夫か」であった。

Chōshun no natsu

    Amūru taigā

      Pino no shisu

In the summer in Changchun

    the Siberian tiger

      Pino was poisoned

Season word: *natsu* (summer; summer)

Manchuria Heavy Industries Development Corporation president

Takasaki Tatsunosuke (1885–1964) cared for animals and

donated his fortune to the new Xinjing (current Changchun) Zoo

in Manchuria. Zoo director Nakamata Mitsushi stated, "His

favorite was a Siberian tiger, Pino. He had no fear of the tiger

and went inside his cage and stroked him." When the Soviet

Army invaded Manchuria on August 9, 1945, the zoo poisoned

Pino and other animals per the Japanese government order.

炎帝や

　　豹の八紘

　　　剥製と化す

えんていや

　　ひょうのはっこう

　　　はくせいとかす

季語　　炎帝（夏を司る神、太陽、夏）

日中戦争中の1941年2月、中国湖北省で日本軍の小隊長成岡

昌久が生後20日の豹の子を保護し、ハチと名付けて可愛がった。

戦局が悪化する中、ハチの安全のため、1942年5月、上野恩賜

動物園に引き取ってもらった（八紘と改名される）。しかし、1943年

8月、同園は戦時危険動物処分を施行し、2歳半の八紘を薬殺し

た（8月18日）。戦後、1946年11月、帰還を果たした成岡は剥製

と化したハチと再会する。ハチを引き取りたいと願い出る成岡に対

し、同園は八紘の剥製を「廃棄物扱い」とする苦肉の策を講じて、

成岡に与えた。こうして、成岡はハチを郷里の高知に連れ帰った。

Entei ya

    hyō no Hakkō

      hakusei to kasu

In the burning summer sun

    the leopard Hakkō

      was mounted

Season word: *entei* ("burning god" sun; summer)

In 1941, Japanese Army sergeant major Naruoka Masahisa (1912–1992) rescued a newborn leopard cub at the warfront in China and named him Hachi. As the war situation worsened in 1942, he sent Hachi to Ueno Zoo for safety, only to find in 1943 that Hakkō (his new name) had been destroyed per the Wartime Disposal of Dangerous Animals order. Hakkō was only two and a half years old and was mounted. Naruoka was repatriated in 1946 and asked the zoo to give him Hakkō's taxidermy. The zoo granted his request and he returned to his hometown with it.

向日葵や

　　飢へと渇きに

　　　象の逝く

ひまわりや

　　うえとかわきに

　　　ぞうのゆく

季語　　向日葵（夏）

1943年8月、上野恩賜動物園は戦時危険動物処分政策の施

行を開始し、園内の「危険動物」を薬殺や撲殺した。3頭のアジ

ア象は、薬の入った餌の匂いを嗅ぎ取り、餌を食べることを拒否

したため、飢え死にさせることとなった。オスのジョンは、8月13

日から水も餌も与えられず、8月29日に死んだ。同動物園では、

飢え死したカバ2頭を含め、計15種・29頭が処分された。

Himawari ya

   ue to kawaka ni

      zō no yuku

The sunflower

   has watched the Asian elephant

      slowly starving to death in the summer heat

Season word: *himawari* (sunflower; summer)

This describes a scene of the Asian elephant John at Ueno Zoo in

August 1943, when the zoo began destroying a total of 29

animals of 15 species per the Wartime Disposal of Dangerous

Animals order. As the three Asian elephants at the zoo smelled

the poison in the food and refused to eat it, the zoo decided to

make them starve to death. They stop feeding food and water to

John on August 13. John died on August 29.

September

Photograph 9. Red spider lily, under Wikimedia Commons license, "Cluster amaryllis close-up," September 19, 2004, https://commons.wikimedia.org/wiki/File:Cluster_amaryllis _close-up.jpg

馬の「赤紙」

　　農夫の嘆き

　　　秋風の聴く

うまのあかがみ

　　のうふのなげき

　　　あきかぜのきく

季語　秋風（秋）

馬の懲兵は人の懲兵に使用された「赤紙」ではなく「青紙」
で伝達されたが、「赤紙」は懲兵の一般用語として使われ
た。アジア・太平洋戦争中には50万頭にも及ぶ日本の馬
が軍馬として大陸や南洋諸島に渡った。農耕に不可欠で
あった馬を供出した農民の苦悩と哀しみは計り知れない。

Uma no "aka gami"

   nōfu no nageki

      aki kaze no kiku

The "red-paper conscription notice" for the horse

   the farmer laments

      and the autumn wind listens

Season word: *aki kaze* (autumn wind; autumn)

The conscription notice for soldiers was called *aka gami*

(red paper) because such notices were written on red paper.

The conscription notices for horses was written on blue

paper, but they were still called *aka gami*, as a generic

name for conscription notices. Horses were an

indispensable workforce for farmers, but they had no way

to refuse the notices. Their despair was immeasurable.

帰還なき

　　馬の出征

　　　　秋の空

きかんなき

　　うまのしゅっせい

　　　　あきのそら

季語　　秋の空（秋）

帰還なき出征を余儀なくされた馬の悲劇と所有者の悲嘆。馬は、

農家にとって使役動物であると同時に家族の一員でもあった。

ある農夫は、可愛がっていた馬「あお」が出征することを娘が悲

しむことを知っていて、娘がまだ寝ている早朝に馬を連れ出し

た。「あお」が戻ってくることはなかった。南洋諸島では、軍馬は

酷暑の中、火山灰の積もる岩山を歩かされた。

Kikan naki

    uma no shussei

        aki no sora

The autumn sky

    watches the horse being conscripted

        without any chance of repatriation

Season word: *aki no sora* (autumn sky; autumn)

During the Asia–Pacific War, as many as 500,000 horses in

Japan were conscripted as military horses and sailed to the

Asian continent and the Pacific Islands, never to return

home. A farm girl was devastated when her family horse,

Ao, was conscripted. She never saw Ao again.

中尊寺

　　つくつく法師の

　　　　お経かな

ちゅうそんじ

　　つくつくぼうしの

　　　　おきょうかな

季語　　つくつく法師（秋）

つくつく法師の鳴き声をお経を唱える僧侶に喩える。蝉は
夏の季語であるが、つくつく法師は、秋に発生する蝉なの
で、秋の季語となる。

Chūson ji

    tsuku tsuku bōshi no

        o kyō kana

In Chūson Temple

    the cicada is chirping

        as if it were chanting the Buddhist sutra

Season word: *tsuku tsuku bōshi* (*hōshi zemi*, Walker's

cicada, *meimuna opalifera*; autumn)

Hōshi zemi literally means "monk cicada." Cicada is a

season word of summer; however, there are different

species of cicada and some appear in autumn. *Tsuku tsuku

bōshi* appears in early autumn and is a season word of

autumn. The venerable Chūson Temple is located in

Hiraizumi, Iwate prefecture.

道端の

　　儚き命

　　　蝉供養

みちばたの

　　はかなきいのち

　　　せみくよう

季語　　蝉（夏・秋）

蝉は、夏の季語であるが、実際には、夏の蝉と秋の蝉がい
る。この句は秋の蝉を詠んだもの。

Michi bata no

hakanaki inochi

semi kuyō

On the street

one finds the dead cicada

and gives a funeral for the ephemeral life

Season word: *semi* (cicada; summer/autumn)

Cicada is a season word of summer; however, there are

different species of cicada and some appear in autumn.

This haiku refers to the autumn cicada.

秋海棠

　　上野の象の

　　　　涙知る

しゅうかいどう

　　うえののぞうの

　　　　なみだしる

季語　　秋海棠（秋）

1945年8月25日、上野恩賜動物園は、アジア象の花子とトンキーに水と餌を与えることをやめた。2頭の象は、飼育員の前で曲芸をして必死に餌をねだった。飼育員の一人、渋谷信吉は、戦後出版した『象の涙』のなかで、「私は耐えきれず、密かに自分の弁当を与えたが、これは、2頭の苦しみを延ばすだけであると悟った」と述懐している。花子は9月11日に餓死した。

Shūkaidō

> Ueno no zō no
>
> namida shiru

The hardy begonia

> knows the tears
>
> of the Asian elephants at Ueno

Season word: *shūkaidō* (hardy begonia; autumn)

On August 25, 1943, Ueno Zoo stopped feeding the two

remaining Asian elephants, Hanako and Tonki (both female).

Out of desperation, they performed antics for public shows in

front of their keepers, begging for food. One of them, Shibuya

Shinkichi, confided in his memoir *Zō no namida* (Tears of

Elephants) that he fed the elephants his own lunch secretly, but

he realized that this would only prolong their misery. Hanako

died on September 11.

白桔梗

　　雌象の死を

　　　　悼みたり

しろききょう

　　めすぞうのしを

　　　　いたみたり

季語　　白桔梗（秋）

1943年9月11日に餓死した花子に続き、9月23日にトンキーが餓死した。水と餌を与えられなくなってから一ヶ月近く生きていた。飼育員の無念と悲しみ。

Shiro kikyō

   mesu zō no shi o

      itami tari

The white balloon flower

   mourns the deaths

      of the female Asian elephants

Season word: *shiro kikyō* (white balloon flower; autumn)

Following the death of the Asian elephant Hanako on

September 11, 1943, the other Asian elephant Tonki died

on September 23. Tonki had lived for almost a month

without water and food. Thereby, all the elephants at Ueno

Zoo had been destroyed. Their keepers were heartbroken.

蟋蟀や

　　翅を震はせ

　　　鎮魂歌

こおろぎや

　　はねをふるわせ

　　　ちんこんか

季語　蟋蟀（秋）

コオロギが羽を震わせて鳴いている様子は、動物を含め

た戦争犠牲者の鎮魂歌を詠っているようである。

Kōrogi ya

    hane o furuwase

        chinkon ka

The cricket

    trembles its wings

        and sings the requiem

Season word: *kōrogi* (cricket; autumn)

The cricket chirping sounds like a requiem for the war victims, both humans and animals.

精霊飛蝗

　　ゴッホの中に

　　　　潜みけり

しょうりょうばった

　　ゴッホのなかに

　　　　ひそみけり

季語　　精霊飛蝗（秋）

2017年11月、ミズーリ州カンザス・シティにあるネルソン・アトキンス美術館は、フィンセント・ファン・ゴッホの油彩画「オリーブ畑」（1889年）の中にショウリョウバッタが偶然に埋め込まれていたと発表した。実際、ゴッホは弟テオに宛てた手紙に、外で絵を描いている時に、ほこりや砂ほこりだけでなく、無数の虫がキャンバスに付いて困ったと記している。

Shōryō batta

Gohho no naka ni

hisomi keri

The grasshopper

was found hidden

in the painting of van Gogh

Season word: *shōryō batta* (Chinese grasshopper, Oriental

longheaded locust; autumn)

In November 2017, the Nelson–Atkins Museum of Art in

Kansas City, Missouri, announced that more than a century

ago, a grasshopper was accidentally embedded in Vincent

van Gogh's painting "Olive Trees (1889)" and thereby the

insect found its way to immortality.

大阪城の

　　菊人形

　　　豹の叫び聞く

おおさかじょうの

　　きくにんぎょう

　　　ひょうのさけびきく

季語　　菊人形（秋）

1943年8月から戦時危険動物処分を施行した東京の上野恩賜動物園に続き、大阪市立動物園は、1943年9月から、エゾグマ、チョウセンオオカミ、ヒョウ、ライオンを含む、計10種・26頭の「危険動物」を処分した。

Osaka jō no

    kiku ningyō

        hyō no sakebi kiku

At Osaka Castle

    chrysanthemum dolls

        heard the cries of the leopard

Season word: *kiku ningyō* (chrysanthemum dolls, dolls

made of chrysanthemums; autumn)

Soon after Ueno Zoo had disposed of its "dangerous

animals" in August 1943, the Osaka City Zoo followed suit

in September, disposing of a total of 26 animals of 10

species, including Ezo brown bears, Korean wolves,

leopards, and lions.

ハイエナや

　　刀一突き

　　　曼珠沙華

ハイエナや

　　かたなひとつき

　　　まんじゅしゃげ

季語　　曼珠沙華（秋）

1943年9月30日、小倉（現在の北九州市）の到津遊園
（現在、到津の森公園）では、政府の戦時危険動物処分
政策に従い、ハイエナを日本刀で刺し殺した。

Haiena ya

    katana hito tsuki

      manjushage

The hyena

    was stabbed with a Japanese sword

      and blood splashed like a red spider lily

Season word: *manjushage* (red spider lily; autumn)

On September 30, 1943, the Itōzu Yūen Zoo in Kokura
(current Kita-Kyūshū City) destroyed a hyena with a
Japanese sword.

October

Photograph 10. School of fish, projected on wall, Kaneno

Misuzu Memorial Museum, Nagato, Yamaguchi prefecture,

August 2012, taken by the author

山茱萸の

　　　色鮮やかに

　　　　　鳥の啄ばむ

さんしゅゆの

　　　いろあざやかに

　　　　　とりのついばむ

季語　　山茱萸（秋）

山茱萸の実は、「秋珊瑚」と言われるほど鮮やかである。

Sanshuyu no

    iro azayaka ni

      tori no tsuibamu

The berries of the Japanese cornelian cherry

    turned vivid red

      and the mountain birds are eating them

Season word: *sanshuyu* (Japanese cornelian cherry, *cornus officinalis*; autumn)

The berries of Japanese cornelian cherry are vivid red so that they are called "autumn coral."

囀りの

　　満ち溢れたり

　　　　ピラカンサ

さえずりの

　　みちあふれたり

　　　　ピラカンサ

季語　ピラカンサ（常盤山査子、トキワサンザシ、秋）

ピラカンサは、その英語名 pyracantha の示す通り（ギリシ

ア語で火、炎という意味の pyr と、棘という意味の

akantha が語源）、燃えるような赤い実をたわわにつける。

Saezuri no

michi afure tari

pirakansa

The bird twittering

is overflowing

the pyracantha

Season word: *pirakansa* (pyracantha, fire thorn; autumn)

As the name implies, pyracantha grows fiery red berries in

abundance.

赤のまま

　　犬の戯れ

　　　　そのままに

あかのまま

　　いぬのたわむれ

　　　　そのままに

季語　　赤のまま(秋)

「あかのまま」は、犬蓼(イヌタデ)の別名。

Aka no mama

    inu no tawamure

        sono mama ni

The Asiatic smartweed

    is letting the dog play in the field

        as it pleases

Season word: *aka no mama* (*lit.*, "as red as it is," Asiatic

smartweed, Oriental lady's thumb; autumn)

Aka no mama is also called *inu tade* (*lit.*, "dog smartweed").

The Asiatic smartweed has red flowers and red berries;

hence the Japanese name, *aka no mama*.

志賀高原

　　靄に浮かびし

　　　母子鹿

しがこうげん

　　もやにうかびし

　　　ははこじか

季語　鹿（秋）

志賀高原は、長野県にある上信越高原国立公園の中心

部を占める高原で、スキーリゾートとして有名。

Shiga Kōgen

    moya ni ukabi shi

        haha ko jika

The doe and her fawns

    loomed in the mist

        of the Shiga Highlands

Season word: *shika* (deer; autumn)

The Shiga Highlands are located in Jōshin'etsu Highlands

Naitonal Park in Nagao prefecture and is a famous ski

resort.

毬栗を

　　避けては歩く

　　　犬と靴

いがぐりを

　　さけてはあるく

　　　いぬとくつ

季語　毬栗（秋）

Iga guri o

sakete wa aruku

inu to kutsu

Avoiding the fallen chestnuts with their burrs

the dog and a pair of shoes

are walking carefully

Season word: *iga guri* (chestnut with its burr; autumn)

秋刀魚の眼

　　彼方の海の

　　　　波の音

さんまのめ

　　かなたのうみの

　　　　なみのおと

季語　秋刀魚（秋）

Sanma no me

    kanata no umi no

        nami no oto

The eyes of the Pacific saury

    look as if they are watching the sea far away

        as if it is listening to the sound of waves far

        away

Season word: *sanma* (Pacific saury, mackerel pike;

autumn)

燕帰る

　　君よ知るや

　　　南の国へ

つばめかえる

　　きみよしるや

　　　みなみのくにへ

季語　　燕帰る（秋）

「君よ知るや南の国」は、ゲーテ（1749年–1832年）の小説『ヴィルヘルム・マイスターの修行時代』の一節。この詞をもとに歌が作曲され、また、「ミニヨン」としてオペラ化されている。

Tsubame kaeru

   kimi yo shiru ya

      minami no kuni e

The swallow is flying back

   to south

      to the tune of "Kennst du das Land"

Season word: *tsubame kaeru* (swallow returns to south; autumn)

"Kennst du das Land" is a line from Book 3, Chapter 1 of *Wilhelm Meister's Apprenticeship* by Jonathan Wolfgang von Goethe (1749–1832). The text begins with "Do you know that country where the citrus blossoms? The orange shines in the dark leaves…" This text was turned into a lied, and into an opera, Mignon.

奈良の秋

　　ましら遊びし

　　　「鴎外の門」

ならのあき

　　ましらあそびし

　　　おうがいのもん

季語　　秋（秋）

「ましら」は、猿の雅語（古語）。森鴎外（1862年–1922年）

が晩年、1917年から1922年、東京・京都・奈良の帝室博

物館総長を務めた時に読んだ短歌、「猿の来（こ）し官舎

の裏の大杉は折れて迹なし常なき世なり」にちなんで。官

舎の跡は、「鴎外の門」として現存する。

Nara no aki

mashira asobi shi

Ōgai no mon

Nara in autumn

the monkeys used to play

at the Ōgai Gate

Season word: *aki* (autumn; autumn)

The Japanese Army surgeon-general and writer Mori Ōgai

(1862–1922) in later years was appointed as Imperial Museum

director-general, overseeing national museums in Tokyo, Nara,

and Kyoto. Reminiscing on his tenure in Nara, he wrote a poem,

"The big cedar behind the government housing / on which

monkeys used to climb / has fallen / and there is no trace of it /

the world is transient." The remains of the government housing

where Mori lived are preserved as "The Ōgai Gate."

秋の色

　　深まりて

　　　　色鳥の来る

あきのいろ

　　ふかまりて

　　　　いろどりのくる

季語　秋（秋）　色鳥（秋）

Aki no iro

    fukamari te

        iro dori no kuru

The autumn color

    deepens

        and the "color birds" are coming

Season words: *aki* (autumn; autumn) and *iro dori* (*lit.*, "color bird"; autumn)

Iro dori refers to migrating birds that fly to Japan in the autumn from Siberia and elsewhere, in order to winter in a warmer climate.

ハロウィーン

　南瓜畑の

　　鴉かな

ハロウィーン

　かぼちゃばたけの

　　からすかな

季語　ハロウィーン（秋）　南瓜（秋）

ハロウィーンにカボチャとカラスは付き物である。

Harowiin

kabocha batake no

karasu kana

On Halloween

the crow rests

in the pumpkin field

Season words: *Harowiin* (Halloween; autumn) and

(pumpkin; autumn)

November

Photograph 11. Cover of *Gon gitsune* (Gon, the Little Fox),

© Kuroi Ken, written by Niimi Nankichi (first published in

1932) and aesthetically and poetically illustrated by Kuroi

Ken (Kaiseisha: Tokyo, 1986), taken by the author.

ごん狐

　　里山の栗

　　　　また実り

ごんぎつね

　　さとやまのくり

　　　　またみのり

季語　狐（冬）

栗は、秋の季語であるが、この句では、季語として使われ
ていない（虚偽の季語）。新見南吉（1913年–1943年）の
『ごん狐』（初出、1932年）へのオマージュ。黒井健の詩情
豊かで繊細かつ美しいイラストレーションによる絵本（198
6年）が偕成社により出版されている。

Gon gitsune

    satoyama no kuri

        mata minori

Reminiscing about Gon, the Little Fox

    the chestnuts of the village mountain

        ripened again

Season word: *kitsune* (fox; winter)

This is a homage to *Gon gitsune* (Gon, the Little Fox, 1932) by

Niimi Nankichi (1913–1943), in which the motherless fox kit

delivered chestnuts and matsutake mushrooms to a villager as a

repentance for his earlier mischief. However, the villager did not

know the real reason why Gon came to his house and shot him,

only belatedly realizing that Gon had brought the food to him.

Kuroi Ken made aesthetic and poetic illustrations for this story

(Kaiseisha: Tokyo, 1986).

母狐

　　はぐれ子探し

　　　月蒼し

ははぎつね

　　はぐれごさがし

　　　つきあおし

季語　狐(冬)

Haha gitsune

hagure go sagashi

tsuki aoshi

The mother vixen

is searching for her kit

under the blue moon

Season word: *kitsune* (fox; winter)

里に入る

　　熊はシングル

　　　マザーなり

さとにいる

　　くまはシングル

　　　マザーなり

季語　熊（冬）

Sato ni iru

kuma wa shinguru

mazā nari

The bear

who sneaks into the village

is a single mother

Season word: *kuma* (bear; winter)

冬薔薇

　　ライオン去りし

　　　伯林の園

ふゆそうび

　　ライオンさりし

　　　ベルリンのその

季語　冬薔薇（ふゆそうび、冬）

第二次世界大戦中、1943年11月22日の連合軍による

ベルリン大空襲で、ベルリン動物園では、ライオン3頭、ゾ

ウ7頭などが死亡した。

Fuyu sōbi

    raion sari shi

        Berurin no sono

In Berlin Zoo

    the lions are gone

        and the winter rose laments

Season word: *fuyu bara* (winter rose; winter)

On November 22, 1943, during World War II, most of the animals in Berlin Zoo, including lions and elephants, were killed in an air raid of the Allied Powers.

笹鳴や

　　大地と光の

　　　　シンコペーション

ささなきや

　　だいちとひかりの

　　　　シンコペーション

季語　　笹鳴（冬）

笹鳴は、ウグイスなどの野鳥の小さい地鳴きのこと。

Sasa naki ya

    daichi to hikari no

        shinkopēshon

The warbling of the wintering birds

    is syncopating

        with the earth and the light

Season word: *sasa naki* (warbling of the wintering birds; winter)

痩せ兎

　　「月のうさぎ」と

　　　　なりにけり

やせうさぎ

　　つきのうさぎと

　　　　なりにけり

季語　兎(冬)

『今昔物語』にも収録されている「月のうさぎ」の伝説。

Yase usagi

    "Tsuki no usagi" to

        nari ni keri

The thin rabbit

    has become

        the Rabbit on the Moon

Season word: *usagi* (rabbit; winter)

This is the folklore tale of the Rabbit on the Moon: A rabbit did not have any food to give to an old traveler. The rabbit threw his body into the fire so that the old man could eat him. A god in heaven was watching this and brought the dead rabbit to the moon. Thus, he became the Rabbit on the Moon. Japanese think that the shadows on the moon are those of the rabbit.

木枯らしや

　　頬を寄せ合ふ

　　　杜の鳩

こがらしや

　　ほほをよせあう

　　　もりのはと

季語　木枯らし（冬）

Kogarashi ya

    hoho o yose au

        mori no hato

The wintry wind blows

    and the pigeons in the shrine

        huddle together cheek to cheek

Season word: *kogarashi* (wintry wind; winter)

冬玄鳥

　　「灰色の王子」と

　　　　眠りたり

ふゆつばめ

　　はいいろのおうじと

　　　　ねむりたり

季語　　冬玄鳥（冬燕、冬）

俳句では、ツバメは玄鳥とも表す。オスカー・ワイルド作

『幸福な王子』にちなんで。「幸福な王子」の銅像の願い

を叶えるために、エジプトに渡ることを諦め、凍え死んだツ

バメを偲んで。「幸福な王子」は、その金メッキを剥がして

貧しい人々に与えたために、「灰色の王子」となった。

Fuyu tsubame

   "haiiro no ōji"

      to nemuri tari

The winter swallow

   rests in peace

      with the "gray prince"

Season word: *fuyu tsubame* (winter swallow; winter)

This is a homage to *The Happy Prince* by Oscar Wilde
(1854–1900). The Happy Prince became the "gray prince"
as he gave away his gold plates.

一茶忌や

　　雀のお宿の

　　　　百九十回忌

いっさきや

　　すずめのおやどの

　　　　ひゃくきゅうじゅっかいき

季語　一茶忌（冬）

俳人、小林一茶（1763年–1828年）の命日は、陰暦の11月19日。2018年は、一茶の190回忌（現代の年数の数え方による）。

Issa ki ya

    suzume no o yado no

        hyaku kyūjukkai ki

On the memorial day of Issa

    the sparrows are conducting

        the 190th memorial service

Season word: *Issa-ki* (anniversary memorial day of Kobayashi Issa's death, November 19 in the lunar calendar; winter)

Kobayashi Issa (1763–1828) was a renowned haiku writer, who expressed genuine compassion for small animals, including sparrows and even small flies.

梟や

　　崕山の無念

　　　描き遺し

ふくろうや

　　かざんのむねん

　　　かきのこし

季語　梟（ふくろう、冬）

渡辺崕山（1793年–1841年）は、三河国田原藩（現在の
愛知県田原市、同県の東南端、渥美半島にある）の家老
であり、画家であった。その命日は11月23日。先見の明
があり、蘭学に通じて、幕府の鎖国・海防政策に反対であ
ったが、その危険を熟知して海防論者を装っていた。しか
し、家宅捜索により開国論の草稿が見つかり、蟄居を命ぜ
られ、その後切腹する。自画像としてフクロウを描いた。

Fukurō ya

    Kazan no munen

        kaki nokoshi

The owl

    drew to depict

        the laments of Kazan

Season word: *fukurō* (owl; winter)

Kazan refers to Watanabe Kazan (1793–1841), a high-ranking

official in Mikawa province (current Tahara, Aichi prefecture).

He was punished by the feudal Tokugawa shogunate government

for his advocacy of abolishing the seclusion policy in favor of an

open-door policy. He was put under house arrest and committed

harakiri suicide on October 11 in the lunar calendar (November

23 in the Gregorian calendar). He drew a self-portrait as an owl.

December

Photograph 12. Japanese red-crowned cranes, under

Wikimedia Commons license, "Red-crowned cranes,

Hokkaido, Japan," February 20, 2011,

https://commons.wikimedia.org/wiki/File:Red-

crowned_Cranes_-_Hokkaido_-

_Japan_S4E4202_(15525814846).jpg

手袋を

　　買ひに来た子は

　　　　尻尾あり

てぶくろを

　　かいにきたこは

　　　　しっぽあり

季語　手袋（冬）

新見南吉の『手袋を買いに』に寄せて。心温まる狐の親子の物語。

Te bukuro o

    kaini kita ko wa

        shippo ari

The child

    who came to buy a pair of mittens

        had a tail

Season word: *te bukuro* (mitten; winter)

This describes a scene in *Tebukuro o kai ni* (Buying Mittens) by Niimi Nankichi (1913–1943). Unlike the sad ending of *Gon, the Little Fox*, by the same author, this is a heart-warming story of a mother vixen and her kit. Japanese folklore has it that foxes can transform themselves into human beings and deceive people.

白銀に

　　消ゆる足跡

　　　　消ゆる兎（う）や

はくぎんに

　　きゆるあしあと

　　　　きゆるうや

季語　　兎（蝦夷雪兎、冬）

エゾユキウサギは寝る前に必ず、跡くらまし（跡消し）を行う
と言われる。周囲の安全を確かめた後、回れ右をして、こ
れまでにできた足跡を少し逆戻りし、それから真横に大き
く跳ぶ。この跡くらましを「兎の止め足」という。従って、「止
め足」があれば、その先にウサギが寝ていることになる。

Hakugin ni

    kiyuru ashiato

      kiyuru u ya

The footsteps of the rabbit

    disappeared in the snow

      and so did the rabbit

Season word: *usagi* (hare, Japanese snow hare; winter)

This describes a unique pattern of footsteps of the Japanese snow hare called "hare's end footsteps." In order to deceive predators before going to sleep, Japanese snow hares deliberately trace back their footsteps left on the snow half way and then leap in a 90-degree angle direction. This way, the hares disguise themselves as being sleeping at the end of the original footsteps, but actually are at the end of the new direction they leapt.

粉雪や

　　大仏の耳に

　　　宿る鳩

こなゆきや

　　だいぶつのみみに

　　　やどるはと

季語　粉雪（冬）

神奈川県にある鎌倉大仏（長谷の大仏）は露坐の大仏である。最近の発掘調査では、鎌倉大仏も元来は、奈良の大仏（東大寺大仏殿の本尊）ののように、大仏殿の中に安置されていたことがわかった。記録によると、大仏殿は、少なくとも二度地震や津波で倒壊したが、1369年の倒壊以降は再建された形跡は見つかっていないという。

Kona yuki ya

    daibutsu no mimi ni

        yadoru hato

The powder snow falls

    and the pigeon takes refuge

        in the ear of the Giant Buddha Statue

Season word: *kona yuki* (powder snow; winter)

The Giant Buddha Statue in Kamakura, Kanagawa

prefecture, is exposed outdoors, unlike the Giant Buddha

Statue at Tōdai Temple in Nara. Research has found that it

actually used to be housed in successive temples, which

were destroyed by earthquakes and tsunamis.

梟や

　　下弦の月の

　　　玄き影

ふくろうや

　　かげんのつきの

　　　くろきかげ

季語　梟（冬）

Fukurō ya

   kagen no tsuki no

      kuroki kage

The owl

   is casting a dark shadow

      on the waning moon

Season word: *fukurō* (owl; winter)

雪の夜は

　　　『鶴の恩返し』

　　　　読み返し

ゆきのよは

　　　つるのおんがえし

　　　　よみかえし

季語　　雪の夜（冬）

日本の民話、『鶴の恩返し』。この話を題材として、木下順
二（1914年–2006年）が戯曲、『夕鶴』（1949年）を書い
た。

Yuki no yo wa

    "Tsuru no on gaeshi"

        yomi kaeshi

On the snowy night

    one is reading

        The Grateful Crane again

Season word: *yuki no yo* (snowy night; winter)

The folklore story of *Tsuru no on gaeshi* (*lit.*, "crane's return of a favor") is a poignant story, which was turned into a play, *Yūzuru* (Twilight Crane, 1949), by the renowned playwright Kinoshita Junji (1914–2006).

大獅子の

　　消えし楽園

　　　鶴の啼く

おおじしの

　　きえしらくえん

　　　つるのなく

季語　　鶴（冬）

名古屋市立東山動物園（陸軍に敷地を接収される）の北王英一園長は戦時危険動物処分に最後まで抵抗したが、遂に、1944年12月13日、処分を迫る地元猟友会員によるライオンの射殺を黙認した（北王は、他の動物園での処分から、薬殺は動物の苦しみを伸ばすことを知っていた）。その後、同園の誇りであったホッキョクグマが射殺されるに及び、計7種・18頭が処分された。翌年6月、北王は落胆と哀しみの余り辞任した。

Ōjishi no

    kieshi rakuen

        tsuru no naku

The crane cries

    in the paradise

        where the lions have disappeared

Season word: *tsuru* (cranes; winter)

This refers to the Higashiyama Zoo in Nagoya on December 13, 1944, where four lions were shot per the Wartime Disposal of Dangerous Animals order. Zoo director Kitaō Hideichi had resisted the order the longest among the zoos nationwide, but a local hunting group urged him to execute the order. In the end he acquiesced (poisoning would prolong the suffering of the animals). The zoo destroyed a total of 18 animals of 7 species, including prized polar bears. Disheartened, Kitaō resigned his position. He kept four Asian elephants secretly. Two of them survived the war and became the only two elephants in Japan.

不忍池

　　少年とハチの

　　　雪合戦

しのばずのいけ

　　しょうねんとハチの

　　　ゆきがっせん

季語　雪合戦（冬）

1925年5月上野英三郎の死後、ハチは浅草に住む八重の親戚に預けられた。岸一敏の『忠犬ハチ公物語』（1934年）によると、ハチはその家の息子と上野公園で雪合戦をしたとあるが、実際は、ハチは1925年の冬には浅草に住んでいない。既にその年の夏、故上野英三郎の庭師小林菊三郎にもらわれて代々木八幡に住んでいだ。

Shinobazu no ike

   shōnen to Hachi no

    yuki gassen

At Shinobazu Pond

   a boy and Hachi-kō

    are playing in a snowball fight

Season word: *yuki gassen* (snowball fight; winter)

This is an image after *Chūken Hachi-kō monogatari* (The Tale of the Loyal Dog Hachi-kō, 1934) by Kishi Kazutoshi. Upon Ueno Hidesaburō's death in May 1925, Hachi was taken to his widow's relative's house in Asakusa, downtown Tokyo. However, in reality, Hachi did not live there that winter. Earlier, in the summer, he was adopted by Ueno Hidesaburō's gardener Kobayashi Kikusaburō and lived in Yoyogi-Hachiman.

雪国の

　　犬の雄叫び

　　　天の聴く

ゆきぐにの

　　いぬのおたけび

　　　てんのきく

季語　雪国（冬）

2017年11月30日に昇天した秋田犬わさおの飼い主、菊谷節子追悼。菊谷を求めて遠吠えをするわさお。

Yuki guni no

    inu no otakebi

        ten no kiku

In snow country

    the dog roared

        and Heaven listened

Season word: *yuki guni* (snow country; winter)

This is a memorial tribute to Wasao's owner, Kikuya

Setsuko in Ajigasawa, Aomori prefecture, who died on

November 30, 2017. Wasao was mourning Kikuya's death

and called to her in Heaven. She was the only person

Wasao opened up to.

細雪

　　主人の声を

　　　　探す犬

ささめゆき

　　あるじのこえを

　　　　さがすいぬ

季語　細雪（冬）

Sasame yuki

    aruji no koe o

        sagasu inu

In fine, light falling snow

    the dog is sniffing in the air

        for the voice of his owner

Season word: *sasame yuki* (fine, light snow; winter)

Wasao missed Kikuya Setsuko so much that he frantically

looked for her everywhere.

秋田犬

　　雪の匂ひに

　　　　何憶ふ

あきたいぬ

　　ゆきのにおいに

　　　　なにおもう

季語　雪（冬）

「お母ちゃん（菊谷節子）はどこに行ってしまったのだろう」
と雪に問うわさお。家人や菊谷の経営していたイカ焼き店
の店員は、菊谷のことを「お母ちゃん」と呼んでいた。

Akita inu

    yuki no nioi ni

        nani omou

Akita-inu

    what is he thinking of

        from the scent of the falling snow?

Season word: *yuki* (snow; winter)

Wasao seemed to be asking the falling snow, "Where on earth did Mom go?" People referred to Kikuya Setsuko as Mom. She watches over Wasao from Heaven forever.

About the author

Mayumi Itoh is a former Professor of Political Science at the University of Nevada, Las Vegas (UNLV). She has also previously taught at Princeton University and Queens College, City University of New York (CUNY), and has written numerous books and academic journal articles. Her book titles include:

–*Globalization of Japan: Japanese Sakoku Mentality and U.S. Efforts to Open Japan* (1998)

–*The Hatoyama Dynasty: Japanese Political Leadership Through the Generations* (2003)

–*Japanese War Orphans in Manchuria: Forgotten Victims of World War II* (2010)

–*Japanese Wartime Zoo Policy: The Silent Victims of World War II* (2010)

–*The Origin of Ping-Pong Diplomacy: The Forgotten Architect of Sino-U.S. Rapprochement* (2011)

–*Pioneers of Sino-Japanese Relations: Liao and Takasaki* (2012)

–*Hachi: The Truth of the Life and Legend of the Most Famous Dog in Japan* (2013)

–*The Origins of Contemporary Sino-Japanese Relations: Zhou Enlai and Japan* (2016)

–*The Making of China's War with Japan: Zhou Enlai and Zhang Xueliang* (2016)

–*The Making of China's Peace with Japan: What Xi Jinping Should Learn from Zhou Enlai* (2017)

–*"Hachi-ko" in Siberia: The True Story of Japanese Prisoners of War and a Dog* (2017)

–*Hachiko: Solving Twenty Mysteries about the Most Famous Dog in Japan* (2017)

–*Eliza Ruhamah Scidmore and Japan: The Life and Journeys to the Far East of the American Woman Who Brought "Sakura" to Washington, D.C.* (2017)

–*Kaneko Misuzu: Life and Poems of A Lonely Princes* (2018)

–*The Japanese Culture of Mourning Whales: Whale Graves and Memorial Monuments in Japan* (2018)

–*Haikus of All Seasons I: The Heavens and the Earth* (2018)

–*Animals and the Fukushima Nuclear Disaster* (2018)

–*Haikus of All Seasons II: Humanity* (2018)